THE INSIDER'S
FAST REVIEW

AP U.S. HISTORY
2021 EXAM

THE ESSENTIAL CONTENT

by LARRY KRIEGER

THE INSIDER'S FAST REVIEW
AP U.S. HISTORY 2021 Exam
THE ESSENTIAL CONTENT

by LARRY KRIEGER

ISBN: 978-1-7368182-0-6
An INSIDER TEST PREP publication of Larry Prep LLC
Art Direction & Design by Station16 (Station16 LLC)

For more Insider resources visit
www.InsiderTestPrep.com

TABLE OF CONTENTS

CHAPTER 3   17
PERIOD 3
1754 – 1800

TIMELINE

The French and Indian War

"No Taxation Without Representation"

Philosophical Foundations of the American Revolution

The American Revolution

The Declaration of Independence

The Influence of Revolutionary Ideals on American Women

The Influence of Revolutionary Ideals on African Americans

Article of Confederation

The Constitutional Convention

The Debate Over Ratification

The Constitution

The New Republic

LOOKING IN-DEPTH

The Consequences of The French And Indian War

The French Alliance

Shays's Rebellion, 1787

The Federalist Papers, 1787

The Alien and Sedition Acts, 1798

CHAPTER 4   **29**

PERIOD 4
1800 – 1848

TIMELINE

Creating a New Nation, 1800 – 1816

The Era of Good Feelings, 1816 – 1824

The Market Revolution in Commerce and Production

The Cult of Domesticity

The Age of Jackson

A New National Culture

The Second Great Awakening

An Age of Reform

Slavery and the Old South

LOOKING IN-DEPTH

The Louisiana Purchase, 1803

Marbury v. Madison, 1803

The Monroe Doctrine, 1823

The Erie Canal, 1825

The Seneca Falls Convention, 1848

CHAPTER 5   45
PERIOD 5
1844 – 1877

TIMELINE
Manifest Destiny

The Mexican-American War

The Wilmot Proviso

The Compromise of 1850

Immigrants and Nativists

The Gathering Storm

The Election of 1860 and Secession

The Emancipation Proclamation

Reconstruction

From Slave to Sharecropper

The Restoration of White Supremacy

LOOKING IN-DEPTH
Polk and Manifest Destiny
The Kansas-Nebraska Act, 1854
Nativism and the Know-Nothing Party
Black Codes, 1866

CHAPTER 6   59

PERIOD 6
1876 – 1898

TIMELINE
Westward Expansion

The "New South"

The Rise of Industrial Capitalism

Labor Unions in the Gilded Age

The New Immigrants

The Revival of Nativist Sentiment

The Social Gospel Movement

Big City Political Machines

The Populist Revolt

LOOKING IN-DEPTH
The Great Railroad Strike, 1877

The Dawes Act, 1887

Plessy v. Ferguson, 1896

The Presidential Election of 1896

Jacob Riis and Jane Addams

CHAPTER 7   75

PERIOD 7
1890 – 1945

CHAPTER 8   **95**

PERIOD 8
1945 – 1980

TIMELINE
The Cold War, 1945 – 1953

The Red Scare and McCarthyism

The 1950s: Prosperity and Conformity

The Civil Rights Movement, 1954 – 1963

The Great Society

The Vietnam War

The Counterculture

Black Power and a New Militancy

The Civil Rights Movement Expands

The Environmental Movement

The 1970s – Political Scandals, Economic Challenges, and

Foreign Policy Crises

LOOKING IN-DEPTH
The Truman Doctrine, 1947

McCarthyism

Brown v. Board of Education, 1954

Gulf of Tonkin Resolution, 1964

Great Society, 1965

ABOUT THE AUTHOR

Larry Krieger earned his B.A. and M.A.T. from the University of North Carolina at Chapel Hill and his M.A. from Wake Forest University. In a career spanning more than four decades, Mr. Krieger taught in urban, rural, and suburban public high schools in North Carolina and New Jersey. He taught a variety of AP subjects including U.S. History, Art History, European History, and American Government. Mr. Krieger has published popular books in all of these subjects.

Mr. Krieger's AP US History courses were renowned for their energetic presentations, commitment to scholarship, and dedication to helping students achieve high AP exam scores. Over 90 percent of Mr. Krieger's APUSH students have scored fives, with the remainder scoring fours. Mr. Krieger has never had an AP student score a one or two.

ACKNOWLEDGEMENTS

Books do not write or publish themselves. They require the work of a number of dedicated and creative peoples.

The typed manuscript must be proofed and assembled into an attractive, well-designed book. As always, Station16 more than met this challenge. Brenton played a key leadership role. He created a distinctive design, offered valuable advice, and managed the project to a successful conclusion. David proofed each page and Ciara shaped the manuscript into flowing layouts.

I would especially like to thank my wife Susan for her indefatigable dedication to this project. As "Editor-in-Chief," Susan read, critiqued, and proofed every page in this book. Her "close reads" spotted misplaced modifiers, passive voice verbs, and unconnected thoughts. Susan gave each chapter a grade and always encouraged me to be "clear and direct."

INTRODUCTION

Preparing for the 2021 APUSH exam will be a formidable challenge. The current situation has forced schools to use a combination of in-class, distant learning, and hybrid approaches. In addition, an unusually harsh winter has forced many districts to cancel classes. The loss of class time is making it difficult for teachers to complete the required APUSH curriculum.

Given these challenges, my students expressed great concern about how to prepare for the 2021 APUSH exam. Should they read and reread their 900-page college textbooks? Or should they spend hours watching YouTube videos?

APUSH textbooks and YouTube videos contain vast amounts of information. Faced with the daunting task of learning huge lists of names, dates, places, and terms, my students encouraged me to write focused review materials that would help them prepare for the 2021 APUSH exam.

MY SEARCH FOR A NEW REVIEW STRATEGY

My search for a successful review strategy began with the AP US History Course and Exam Description (CED) book. It provides a detailed, 237-page presentation of the content and skills that are the focus of the APUSH course and exam. Topics covered in the CED book are regularly tested. Topics not in the CED book will NOT be tested. Unfortunately, many review books and videos ignore this fundamental fact.

APUSH test writers use the CED to generate questions for each exam. We now have a very extensive body of authentic APUSH questions. My analysis of these questions AND their answers led me to two key conclusions. First, test writers never write questions asking for specific names, dates, places, and definitions. Second, the test writers focus their attention on historic developments, trends, and patterns. For example, APUSH questions will not ask a student to name battles, commanders, or treaties between American Indians and the U.S. government. But they do expect students to know that these conflicts began over settlers' incursions onto American Indian lands and that the treaties usually lasted a short time.

A BOLD NEW APPROACH

My analysis of the CED book and APUSH questions and answers led me to a bold new approach. *Fast Review: The Essential Content* is designed to live up to its title. My new book provides you with a carefully organized presentation of the key developments, trends, and patterns you must know to achieve a high score on your APUSH exam. There are no fun facts and trivial topics. Everything in *Fast Review* is taken from the CED and APUSH questions and answers.

A STRATEGIC ORGANIZATION

Fast Review, The Essential Content contains ten chapters and a Glossary of key terms. Chapters 1 – 9 are devoted to the nine required time periods covered in the CED. My topical headings closely follow those used in the CED. The numbered points under each topic identify key developments, trends, and patterns regularly tested on APUSH exams. Chapters 2 – 8 conclude with one-page essays that provide an in-depth look at an important topic. For example, the in-depth feature in Chapter 4 describes how the Erie Canal contributed to the market revolution transforming the American economy.

APUSH exams stress the importance of making comparisons between historic events and developments. This skill plays a significant role in a number of multiple-choice and short-answer questions. Chapter 10 provides a unique chronological description of key historic comparisons that have generated a number of APUSH questions. For example, a widespread fear of aliens and communist subversives created a climate of paranoia that led to the Red Scares following World War I and World War II.

Fast Review: The Essential Content concludes with a Glossary that defines and explains the importance of 45 key terms. This short but essential list focuses on terms that have actually generated APUSH questions. There is no reason to spend valuable review time memorizing hundreds of terms in the Glossary of a typical textbook.

YOU CAN DO IT!

College textbooks and YouTube videos are like battleships loaded with information. In contrast, *Fast Review: The Essential Content* is a fast and nimble attack boat, armed with the information you need to know to achieve a high score on the 2021 APUSH exam.

The 2021 APUSH exam will be a challenge. But you will be up to it. My students are becoming more and more confident and so will you. You can do it!

THE 2021 APUSH EXAM FORMATS

The College Board will offer students a choice of two formats for the 2021 APUSH exam:

THE PAPER EXAM: 3 HOURS AND 15 MINUTES LONG

1. Multiple Choice: 55 questions, 55 minutes, 40 percent of the exam score.
2. Short Answer: 3 questions, 40 minutes, 20 percent of the exam score. The first two short answer questions are mandatory. However, you have a choice between two prompts for the third question.
3. Document-Based Question: 1 question, 60 minutes, 25 percent of the exam score.
4. Long Essay: 1 question, 40 minutes, 15 percent of the exam score. You will have a choice among three prompts for your long essay.

THE DIGITAL EXAM: 3 HOURS AND 15 MINUTES LONG

1. Multiple Choice: 55 questions, 55 minutes, 40 percent of the exam score.
2. Short Answer: 3 mandatory questions, 40 minutes, 20 percent of the exam score.
3. Document-Based Question: 1 question, 60 minutes, 25 percent of the exam score.
4. Short Essay: 2 mandatory questions, 40 minutes, 15 percent of the exam score.

THE APUSH SCALE

Many students assume the APUSH exam contains 100 points and that they need 90 points for a 5, 80 points for a 4, and 70 points for a 3. This common belief is incorrect. The APUSH exam actually contains 140 points. On the 2019 exam students needed 106 points for a 5, 90 points for a 4, and 72 points for a 3. Here is the official APUSH exam score conversion chart for the 2019 APUSH exam:

SCORE RANGE	AP SCORE	MINIMUM PERCENT CORRECT
106–140	5	76 percent
90–105	4	65 percent
72–89	3	52 percent
53–71	2	38 percent
0–52	1	0–37 percent

This chart is not a misprint. You can earn a 3 by correctly answering just 52 percent of the questions, a 4 by answering 65 percent of the questions, and a 5 by answering 76 percent of the questions.

The APUSH scale underscores the importance of the strategic approach used in this book. You do not have to memorize information in a textbook or a series of YouTube videos. Instead, you can achieve a high score by becoming familiar with the developments, trends, and patterns described in this book.

CHAPTER 1
PERIOD 1
1491 – 1607

TIMELINE

38,000 – 12,000 B.C.   Ancient hunters migrate to America

2500 B.C.   Corn developed as a staple crop in central Mexico

1000 C.E.   Corn cultivation reaches the Eastern Woodlands

900 – 1200 C.E.   Hopi and Zuni build planned towns

1200   Cahokia city-empire along the Mississippi

1434   Portuguese explore coast of Sub-Saharan Africa

1492   Columbus's first voyage to the Americas

1502   First enslaved Africans transported to Caribbean islands

1521   Hernan Cortes defeats the Aztecs

1542   Bartolome' de las Casas's *A Short Account of the Destruction of the Indies*

1585   English colony at Roanoke Island

THE FIRST AMERICANS

1. By about nine thousand years ago, people could be found from Alaska to the southernmost tip of South America.

2. Indigenous peoples populations settled across the vast expanse of North America. Over time, they developed distinctive complex societies by adapting to and transforming their diverse environments.

3. Native Americans spoke hundreds of distinct languages. They did not know they were a common category of people until named and treated so by the European invaders.

4. The early peoples of North America lived in families that were part of larger clans. They lived in village communities, divided labor by gender,

and shared a strong sense of spirituality. They believed that every element in nature contained some measure of spiritual power.

5. Native peoples developed a mathematically based calendar, constructed irrigation systems, built multi-family dwellings, and lived in cities inhabited by 100,000 or more people.

6. The early peoples did not develop wheeled vehicles, waterwheels, or a tradition of private property rights. Native Americans viewed land and water as communal possessions that could not be owned or traded.

7. Indians living in central Mexico pioneered the cultivation of maize, beans, and squash. As these farming techniques spread northward, they enabled Native Americans to develop settled farming communities.

8. Between 700 and 1200 C.E.., maize, beans, and squash became integral parts of the Native American diet.

9. The abundant natural resources of the Pacific Northwest supported a relatively dense population. Waterways teemed with fish and dense forests supplied game, berries, and wood for housing and boats. People such as the Kwakiutl celebrated their abundance by carving magnificent totems as symbols of the ancestral spirits that guided each family.

10.   The Southwest was much drier than the Pacific Northwest. The Hopi collected rainwater in rock cisterns and carefully parceled it out to their fields. People throughout the region lived in multi-story houses made of adobe. They coaxed crops of corn, beans, melons, and squash, from the sun-parched but fertile soil.

11.   The Great Plains are flat open grasslands extending from the Rocky Mountains to the Mississippi River. Huge buffalo herds once roamed these grasslands. The Pawnee were farmers who planted corn, squash, and beans. Once the plants were strong the entire Pawnee tribe packed up for the spring buffalo hunt. On the hunt, the Pawnee lived in tepees, portable houses made of buffalo skins.

12.   Hardwood forests dominated the Eastern Woodlands, a vast region stretching from the Great Lakes and St. Lawrence River in the north to the Gulf of Mexico in the south. The tribes in this region lived in semi-permanent villages built in forest clearings. They blended agriculture with hunting and gathering.

COLUMBUS AND THE SPANISH CONQUISTADORES

1. Columbus and other Spanish sea captains hoped to chart a new ocean route to Asia. Instead, they discovered two vast new continents.

2. Spanish conquistadores like Cortez and Pizarro hoped to topple the Aztec and Inka empires in order to seize power and wealth.

3. Spanish missionaries came to the New World to promote Christianity.

THE COLUMBIAN EXCHANGE

1. The COLUMBIAN EXCHANGE refers to the exchange of plants, animals, microbes, and peoples between the New World, Europe, and Africa in the 150 years following the discovery of America in 1492.

2. The Columbian Exchange set in motion a series of profound changes that brought catastrophic losses to Native Americans, immense suffering to West Africans, and unprecedented prosperity to Western Europeans.

3. Nutritious New World foods such as maize, potatoes, and tomatoes improved European diets, thus stimulating population growth and economic activity. At the same time, the influx of New World gold and silver facilitated economic growth. These powerful forces contributed to the rising prosperity of the merchant class in Western Europe.

4. European microbes caused epidemics that led to a catastrophic decline in Native American populations. Demographers estimate that 40 to 100 million people lived in the Americas in 1491. The figure plummeted to an estimated 8 million people in 1600.

THE ENCOMIENDA SYSTEM

1. An ENCOMIENDA was a license granted by the Spanish to royal officials to extract labor and tribute from native peoples living in specified areas.

2. The Spanish created the encomienda system to organize and exploit Native American labor. The encomienda system began in the Caribbean and spread to Mexico.

3. The encomienda system allowed Spanish colonial economies to marshal Native American labor to support plantation-based agriculture and extract precious metals.

4. Although the native peoples were not legally slaves, ruthless planters nevertheless created a brutal system of forced labor that led to many abuses.

5. The inhumanity of the system appalled Dominican priest Bartolome' de las Casas. He renounced his encomienda and became an eloquent critic of how the Spanish mistreated native peoples.

NEW SPAIN

1. Spanish authorities attempted to exercise a significant degree of administrative control over New Spain. The royal council in Madrid divided their American empire into two immense regions known as viceroyalties. The king appointed a viceroy to govern each region. However, the great distance between Madrid and New Spain enabled colonial authorities to delay, frustrate, and sometimes evade royal orders.

2. As disease and warfare reduced their numbers, the native population could not meet the Spanish demand for a large body of captive laborers. By the early 1500s, the Spanish began to import enslaved Africans to labor on Caribbean sugar plantations and in Peruvian silver mines. About 300,000 enslaved Africans arrived in New Spain between 1500 and 1650.

3. Women comprised less than one-third of the total number of Spaniards who settled in the New World. As a result, many male emigrants married Native American women. Their racially mixed offspring became known as mestizos.

4. The Spanish developed a race-based society. New Spain's high rate of intermarriage produced a racially mixed population of Europeans, Africans, and Native Americans.

5. Spanish colonists were devout Catholics. They did not leave Spain to seek greater religious freedom.

6. Jesuit and Franciscan priests waged a vigorous campaign to convert Native Americans to the Catholic faith.

7. The Spanish discovered and colonized Florida. The presence of the Spanish in this region illustrates the growing competition between European powers in the Americas.

CHAPTER 2
PERIOD 2
1607 – 1754

TIMELINE

1607	English establish Jamestown
1608	French establish Quebec
1619	First Africans arrive in Virginia
1619	House of Burgesses convenes
1620	Pilgrims found Plymouth
1630	Puritans found Massachusetts Bay Colony
1636	Puritans banish Roger Williams
1637	Puritans condemn Anne Hutchinson for heresy
1651	First English Navigation Acts
1675	King Philip's War
1676	Bacon's Rebellion
1680	Pueblo Revolt
1681	William Penn granted Pennsylvania charter
1730	Beginning of First Great Awakening
1754	Beginning of the French and Indian War

NEW FRANCE

1. The French explored the Great Lakes and the Mississippi River Valley.

2. French fur traders and trappers dominated the lucrative fur trade. Beaver skins were France's major "money crop." In the best years, traders bought and sold over 100,000 beaver skins. For example, in 1693, a fleet of 400 Indigenous canoes brought furs to French traders in Montreal.

3. French fur traders developed a cooperative relationship with Native American tribes. Unlike the English settlers, they did not build plantations and farms on lands claimed by Native Americans.

THE CHESAPEAKE COLONIES

1. The Chesapeake colonies included Virginia and Maryland.

2. Jamestown was founded by the Virginia Company, a joint-stock company dedicated to making a profit.

3. Fertile soil, a warm climate, abundant rainfall, and a long growing season enabled Chesapeake planters to successfully cultivate tobacco as a cash crop.

4. Tobacco required a large and inexpensive labor force. Virginia planters initially turned to English indentured servants. They comprised about three-fourths of the 120,000 people who immigrated to the Chesapeake during the seventeenth century.

5. Discontented frontier farmers, many of whom had been indentured servants, rebelled against the arbitrary rule of Governor Berkeley and the haughty class of wealthy planters he represented.

6. Led by Nathaniel Bacon, the rebels captured and burned Jamestown. But Bacon's sudden death from dysentery enabled Berkeley to regain the upper hand and crush the rebellion.

7. Bacon's Rebellion exposed tensions between the wealthy planters and the poor, former indentured servants. The threat of violence encouraged alarmed Chesapeake planters to replace unruly indentured servants with enslaved Africans.

8. The number of enslaved Africans in Virginia rose from 300 in 1650 to over 100,000 in 1750. Strict laws codified slavery as a system of race-based, inherited, and perpetual bondage. Virginia thus developed a rigid racial system that contrasted with the racially mixed society in New Spain.

THE NEW ENGLAND COLONIES

1. The New England colonies included Massachusetts Bay, New Hampshire, Connecticut, and Rhode Island. These colonies were founded by a relatively homogenous group of Puritan settlers who fled religious persecution in England.

2. The Puritans had a powerful sense of mission. In his famous "City Upon a Hill" sermon, John Winthrop expressed the Puritan belief that they had a

special pact with God to build a "city upon a hill" that would serve as an ideal Christian commonwealth.

3. Although the Puritans came to America for religious freedom, they did not tolerate outspoken religious dissenters. For example, Puritan authorities banished Anne Hutchinson for her unorthodox religious views and Roger Williams for his unorthodox political views.

4. The Puritans settled in families and rarely intermarried with Native Americans. They typically lived in small, tight-knit communities centered around a meetinghouse.

5. The New England environment featured long, cold winters, stony soils, and relatively brief growing seasons. Farmers nonetheless cultivated a healthy mix of crops that included wheat, rye, maize, potatoes, and beans. The dense hardwood forests produced fine lumber for ships.

6. Familiar forms of British institutions such as town meetings and representative assemblies took root in the New England colonies.

THE MIDDLE ATLANTIC COLONIES

1. The Middle Atlantic colonies included New York, New Jersey, Pennsylvania, and Delaware.

2. Geography blessed the region with broad, navigable rivers and deep natural harbors that promoted commerce and diverse business opportunities.

3. Middle Atlantic farmers grew abundant crops of wheat, corn, and other grains. Enterprising merchants shipped the region's surplus grains to the sugar plantations in the Caribbean. Killing fall frosts meant they would not be tempted to cultivate tobacco.

4. William Penn founded Pennsylvania as a refuge for Quakers. Quakers were religious dissenters who believed that all people were equal since every individual possessed a spiritual inner light. Quakers were pacifists who refused to bear arms. They advocated religious toleration, opposed slavery, and allowed women to speak publicly in religious meetings.

THE BRITISH WEST INDIES COLONIES

1. Sugar plantations dominated economic life in the British West Indies. Sugar required expansive equipment, a large labor force, and extensive land holdings.

2. The West Indian sugar economy created a society consisting of a fabulously wealthy planter elite, a vast population of enslaved Africans, and a small

number of free whites. The scarcity of land on small islands forced many whites to leave the British West Indies.

TRANS-ATLANTIC TRADE

1. The exchange of goods and labor between Africa, the Americas, and Europe led to the emergence of a trans-Atlantic economy.

2. Technological advances in navigation and ship construction allowed for improved transportation, communication, and trade volume across the Atlantic.

3. MERCANTILISM was a British economic policy designed to achieve a favorable balance of trade by exporting more goods than it imported. In order to achieve this goal, Great Britain purchased raw materials from its American colonies and then sold them more expensive manufactured goods.

4. Growing Atlantic trade led Parliament to enact a series of Navigation Acts intended to integrate the American colonies into a coherent imperial structure based on mercantilist principles.

5. European wars prevented Great Britain from rigorously enforcing the Navigation Acts. During a period of extended "salutary neglect," colonial merchants successfully evaded burdensome mercantile regulations.

NATIVE AMERIANS AND THE COLONISTS

1. The New England Puritans and the Chesapeake colonists followed a similar pattern of interaction with Native Americans.

2. Colonists in both regions began by establishing peaceful relations with the indigenous peoples. However, tensions quickly arose as the expanding colonial population placed relentless pressure on tribal lands and resources. At the same time, colonists began to view Native Americans as "savages" who practiced "cruel and barbarous" religions.

3. Conflicts over land and culture led to a series of costly wars. In Virginia, the Powhatan confederacy launched bloody attacks that failed to dislodge the English colonists. At the same time, New Englanders successfully defeated a coalition led by a Native American leader named Metacomet, also known as King Philip. The brutal raids claimed the lives of 1,000 settlers and at least 4,000 Native Americans. The clashes in Virginia and New England left the Native Americans a broken and defeated people.

SLAVERY IN THE SOUTHERN COLONIES

1. Geography played a crucial role in the growth of slavery in the Southern colonies. Fertile land, a warm climate, abundant rainfall, and a long growing season enabled planters in Virginia and South Carolina to grow tobacco, rice, and indigo as cash crops.

2. Tobacco and rice required a large supply of inexpensive labor. Enslaved Africans provided a number of economic advantages. Unlike indentured servants, slaves were compelled to work for the duration of their lives.

3. By the mid-1700s, a small but powerful group of wealthy planters dominated Southern society. Although the majority of white families in the South did not own slaves, they did aspire to become slave owners. Impoverished whites felt superior to enslaved Africans, thus providing social support for slavery.

4. Few seventeenth- and early eighteenth-century white colonists questioned human bondage as either morally unacceptable or a contradiction of their belief in liberty.

5. In 1705, the Virginia General Assembly enacted laws codifying slavery as a system of race-based, inherited, and perpetual bondage. The Virginia statutes provided models for similar laws in other Southern states.

6. A combination of economic necessity, legal codes, and social support enabled slavery to develop in Virginia in the period from 1607 to 1750.

COLONIAL SOCIETY AND CULTURE

1. The FIRST GREAT AWAKENING was a religious revival that stressed emotion as a way to achieve personal salvation. In contrast, the ENLIGHTENMENT was an intellectual movement that stressed human reason as a way to discover the natural laws that regulated both the universe and human society.

2. George Whitefield was a British evangelist and charismatic preacher who traveled to North America. He conducted a widely attended series of dramatic open-air sermons that enthralled Great Awakening audiences from Georgia to Maine. Whitefield's career illustrates the growing importance of trans-Atlantic cultural exchanges between Great Britain and its North American colonies.

3. Both the First Great Awakening and the Enlightenment challenged traditional authority. The First Great Awakening challenged the authority of the "Old

Light" Puritan and Anglican ministries. The Enlightenment challenged the authority of the British Crown and royal officials in the colonies.

4. The First Great Awakening led to the emergence of a number of Protestant Evangelical sects. Since no one sect was strong enough to dominate the others, the different sects had to tolerate each other. This led to support for freedom of religion in America.

5. The Enlightenment's concepts of reason and natural rights reinforced the colonial idea that the colonies could govern themselves. The right to self-governance is stressed in the opening paragraph of the Declaration of Independence.

LOOKING IN-DEPTH

JOHN WINTHROP'S CITY UPON A HILL SERMON, 1630

I'd like you to imagine that you and your family are part of a large contingent of over 700 Puritans who left England in 1630, headed to found the Massachusetts Bay Colony in New England. As fate would have it, you are on board the flagship vessel, the *Arabella*. You have been summoned by your leader, John Winthrop, to hear a sermon.

Winthrop began by admonishing his fellow Puritans that "we must consider that we shall be a city upon a hill, the eyes of all peoples are upon us."

What did Winthrop mean by the phrase "city upon a hill?" And how could "the eyes of all peoples" be upon a tiny group of Puritans sailing west in the vast Atlantic Ocean? Winthrop used the phrase "city upon a hill" to remind the Puritans that they had a special covenant with God. They were not like the settlers at Jamestown who were hoping to find gold and make a profit for their joint-stock company. The Puritans were embarking on a very different mission. Their goal was to build a model Christian society. Their "city upon a hill" would then serve as a beacon of righteousness that would inspire reforms in the Church of England. That is why Winthrop believed that "the eyes of all people are upon us."

So why should you remember Winthrop's "City Upon a Hill" sermon? Winthrop's famous sermon is often cited as the first example of American exceptionalism, the belief that America is inherently different from other nations. It is interesting to note that Winthrop's "City Upon a Hill" sermon and the nineteenth-century concept of Manifest Destiny both assumed that America had a divinely sanctioned mission to create a model society.

BACON'S REBELLION, 1676

Our story begins with frustrated and angry small farmers living in Virginia in 1676. The yeoman farmers had good reason to be angry. Many had been indentured servants. It is very important to remember that between 1607 and 1676 indentured servants comprised the chief source of agricultural labor in the Chesapeake colonies of Virginia and Maryland.

Once they earned their freedom, the former indentured servants were frustrated by falling tobacco prices, rising taxes, and dwindling opportunities to purchase fertile land near navigable rivers.

Led by Nathaniel Bacon, the discontented yeoman farmers rebelled against the arbitrary rule of Governor Berkeley and the haughty class of wealthy planters he represented. For a while it looked like Bacon's Rebellion might succeed. The rebels even managed to capture and burn down Jamestown. But Bacon's sudden death from dysentery enabled Governor Berkeley to regain the upper hand. He promptly crushed the rebellion and hung over 20 rebels, calling them "a rabble of the basest sort of people."

So why should you remember Bacon's Rebellion? The rebellion exposed tensions between poor former indentured servants and the wealthy tidewater gentry. Bacon's Rebellion did not overthrow Virginia's wealthy planter aristocracy. But it did much to encourage the Virginia planters to replace indentured servants with slaves imported from Africa. Bacon's Rebellion is thus a very important link in the chain of events that led to the growth of slavery in the South.

THE PUEBLO REVOLT, 1680

Visitors to Statutory Hall in Washington, D.C. are greeted by 100 statues, two from each state in the Union. Most of statues commemorate the contributions of presidents, senators, and governors. However, one statue from New Mexico is very different from the others. It is dedicated to a proud Pueblo religious leader named Pope'.

During the 17th Century, the Spanish gradually gained control over New Mexico and the Pueblo people. The Spanish disrupted the Pueblo's traditional culture by forcing them to labor on encomiendas and worship in Spanish missions. By 1680, the Pueblo were on the brink of losing their cultural identity.

Pope' was described by contemporaries as "a fierce and dynamic" leader who deeply resented the Spanish rulers. His message was simple: expel the Spanish and return to the old ways of life that had given the Pueblo peace, prosperity, and independence. Led by Pope', the Pueblo rose in revolt in August 1680. The Pueblo Revolt succeeded in driving the Spanish out of New Mexico.

The Pueblo Revolt did not bring peace and prosperity to the Pueblo. A drought destroyed their crops and internal divisions weakened their ability to resist both the Spanish and other nearby tribes. In addition, Pope' died in 1688 thus robbing the Pueblo of their inspirational leader. Just four years after Pope's death, the Spanish began a successful reconquest of the Pueblos.

So why should you remember the Pueblo Revolt? Although their independence from Spanish rule proved to be short-lived, the revolt had important enduring consequences. The Spanish no longer tried to eradicate the Pueblo's culture and religion. Pope's leadership was thus not in vain. Over the next centuries, New Mexico became a blend of both Spanish and Pueblo cultures.

THE FIRST GREAT AWAKENING, 1730-1750

Benjamin Franklin was normally a secular person who prided himself on being an Enlightened thinker who valued science and reason. But after listening to the Anglican minister George Whitefield deliver a passionate sermon in Philadelphia, Franklin proclaimed that "it seemed as if all the world was going religious."

Franklin's assessment was correct. During the 1730s and 1740s a religious revival known as the First Great Awakening swept across all 13 colonies. The revival began with Jonathan Edwards in New England and reached a peak with George Whitefield's repeated visits to North America.

Whitefield drew huge, enthusiastic crowds who embraced his message of hope and salvation. Like other First Great Awakening preachers, Whitefield deemphasized ceremony and ritual. Instead, he preached that the true value of a person lies in the quality of his or her moral behavior. Rather than being predestined for damnation, men and women could save themselves by repenting and performing good works.

So why should you remember the First Great Awakening? The First Great Awakening had a number of important consequences that are frequently tested on the APUSH exam. It challenged the "Old Light" Puritan ministers, strengthened the Baptist and Methodist denominations, involved more women in church congregations, and brought Christianity to the African slaves. In addition, when Whitefield opened his sermons by addressing "all of you, high and low, rich and poor," he stressed a new notion of egalitarian democracy in which a person's moral behavior counted for more than his or her economic class. It was just a short step from the right of all people to actively participate in their religion to the right of all people to actively participate in their government.

MERCANTILISM

In an address to Parliament on March 22, 1775, Edmund Burke marveled at the twelve-fold expansion of Britain's commerce with its North American colonies since 1700. Burke cited a "wise and salutary neglect" as the prime factor responsible for America's booming commercial prosperity.

It is important to note that Burke deliberately chose to ignore Britain's official economic policy known as mercantilism. Like other European nations, the British adopted mercantilist polices designed to promote a favorable balance of trade with their colonies. Beginning in 1651, Parliament passed a series of Navigation Acts to regulate all trade with its colonies. For example, the Navigation Act of 1696 required all colonial goods to be transported in ships built in England, Ireland, and the North American colonies.

On first glance, the Navigation Acts appeared to strictly implement Britain's mercantilist principles. However, Parliament did not rigorously enforce the acts. During the period of what Burke correctly called "salutary neglect," mercantilist restrictions and British salutary neglect existed simultaneously.

The combination of mercantilist Navigation Acts and salutary neglect helped create a thriving colonial economy. The growth of trade noted by Burke fostered the increased availability of consumer goods in the British North American colonies. At the same time, colonial efforts to avoid mercantilist restrictions helped foster the growth of a lucrative system of smuggling. For example, New England merchants profited from illegally exporting fish and lumber to French possessions in the Caribbean.

So why should you remember mercantilism? Britain's mercantilist system was intended to subordinate the colonial economy to that of the mother country. However, the policy of salutary neglect enabled colonial merchants to evade most mercantilist regulations. As a result, the colonists developed a spirit of independence that first expressed itself when Parliament enacted the Stamp Act in 1765.

CHAPTER 3
PERIOD 3
1754 – 1800

TIMELINE

1763   Great Britain wins the French and Indian War

1765   Parliament enacts the Stamp Act

1770   Boston Massacre

1773   Boston Tea Party

1776   Congress declares Independence

1781   The Articles of Confederation were ratified

1787   Constitutional Convention meets

1789   George Washington becomes the first president

THE FRENCH AND INDIAN WAR

1. The French and Indian War began as a struggle for control of the upper Ohio River.

2. The French and Indian War ended French power in North America. Under the terms of the Treaty of Paris of 1763, the British North American empire now stretched from the Atlantic coast to the Mississippi River and from Canada to the Gulf of Mexico. Colonists celebrated peace by praising their mother country and optimistically predicting the beginning of a prolonged period of peace and prosperity.

3. Native Americans did not celebrate the British victory. The war left them in a vulnerable position by ending their lucrative trade networks with French fur traders. It also prevented tribal leaders from using shifting military alliances to negotiate favorable agreements by playing the French and English against each other.

"NO TAXATION WITHOUT REPRESENTATION"

1. The French and Indian War doubled Britain's national debt. Indignant royal officials complained that the average person in Great Britain had a debt 45 times as great as that of the average colonist.

2. Parliament enacted the Stamp Act to assert royal control and to raise revenue to help pay for British troops in America.

3. The Stamp Act provoked a contentious debate over Parliament's right to tax its American colonies.

4. British leaders argued that Parliament was based upon a system of virtual representation in which each member represented the interests of all Englishmen, including the colonists.

5. The colonists rejected virtual representation. They argued that as Englishmen they could only be taxed by their elected representatives.

6. The Stamp Act sparked a series of popular boycotts, mob protests, and violence against royal officials.

7. The Boston Massacre and the Boston Tea Party played important roles in escalating tensions between the colonists and British authorities.

PHILOSOPHICAL FOUNDATIONS OF THE AMERICAN REVOLUTION

1. REPUBLICANISM is the belief that government should be based on the consent of the governed. The colonists had a long-standing tradition of making local decisions in town meetings and in representative assemblies such as the House of Burgesses.

2. Key republican values included an emphasis on individual talent over hereditary privilege, opposition to standing armies, belief in the virtue of agrarian life, and a firm commitment to self-government by locally elected representatives.

3. Republican ideas shaped the American revolutionary movement by providing a common ideological framework that bound together the Northern and Southern colonies.

4. The political ideas of British writers such as John Locke inspired colonists to rethink the rights of British subjects. For example, in *Common Sense*, Thomas Paine defended republican principles while denouncing monarchy as a form of government that threatened people's liberty. Paine's widely read pamphlet illustrates the power of ideas to influence American revolutionary thought.

5. Paine argued that independence was inevitable since a prosperous and growing continent could not be permanently tied to a small and distant island. Paine concluded by exhorting the colonists to declare independence and "begin the world over again." Paine's widely read pamphlet illustrates the power of ideas to influence American revolutionary thought.

THE DECLARATION OF INDEPENDENCE

1. A growing commitment to republican values caused many colonists to accuse the British government of violating their natural rights and to support self-government. Although some colonists remained loyal to the Crown, a determined group of Patriots overcame their opposition and declared independence from Great Britain.

2. The Declaration of Independence marked a significant turning point in American history. Prior to the declaration, the colonists were still subjects of the British Crown. The Declaration created a new American identity by transforming a debate over taxes into a fight for independence.

3. The Declaration has had enduring consequences that transcended its initial purpose. Jefferson did not base his revolutionary argument upon the narrow rights of Englishmen. Instead, he drew upon the ideas of John Locke and other Enlightenment writers to base his argument upon universal principles derived from "the Laws of Nature" and "Nature's God."

4. Although not originally fulfilled, Jefferson's ringing statement that "all men are created equal" became an integral part of the American dream.

THE AMERICAN REVOLUTION

1. The pivotal American victory at Saratoga persuaded France to declare war on Great Britain and openly aid the American cause.

2. The French king Louis XVI did not support America because he was sympathetic to republican values. Instead, he was motivated by a desire to avenge his country's humiliating defeat in the French and Indian War.

3. During the Revolutionary War, Native Americans allied with the British or the Americans depending upon their own self-interests.

4. The Treaty of Paris officially recognized American independence and sovereignty over territories extending from the Mississippi River in the west, to the Great Lakes in the north, and to Spanish Florida in the south.

THE INFLUENCE OF REVOLUTIONARY IDEALS ON AMERICAN WOMEN

1. Abigail Adams's famous plea to "Remember the Ladies" demonstrated that at least some colonial women were aware of the discrepancy between their subordinate legal status and the republican ideal of equality.

2. Women's subordinate legal status remained unchanged. For example, American women still could not form a contract, buy or sell property, serve on a jury, hold a political office, or vote.

3. Although women's subordinate legal position remained unchanged, the new republic required well-informed citizens. This need helped give rise to a new ideal of American wives that historians now call REPUBLICAN MOTHERHOOD. According to its advocates, republican mothers have the important responsibility of becoming exemplary parents who would raise their children to become virtuous citizens. Women would thus play a vital role in shaping America's moral character.

THE INFLUENCE OF REVOLUTIONARY IDEALS ON AFRICAN AMERICANS

1. The American Revolution created a new ideal of a society based upon liberty and human rights. This language of liberty did not fall upon deaf ears in the North. Motivated by political and religious opposition to slavery, Mid-Atlantic and New England states initiated a "First Emancipation" by enacting laws eliminating slavery.

2. The Continental Congress further underscored the growing antislavery sentiment in the North. Enacted in 1787, the Northwest Ordinance contained the spread of slavery by prohibiting it in the territories comprising the Old Northwest. As a result, slavery rapidly became identified as a distinctive Southern institution.

ARTICLES OF CONFEDERATION

1. The Articles of Confederation created a "firm league of friendship" that could not exercise power independent of the states. For example, Congress could not tax the people, regulate trade, or raise an army. Congress could only ask the states for money and soldiers.

2. The limited national government consisted only of a unicameral legislature. The government lacked executive and legislative branches.

3. The Northwest Ordinance of 1787 provided an orderly procedure for territories to become new states on an equal basis with the original 13 states. It was the first national law to bar slavery from a specific region.

THE CONSTITUTIONAL CONVENTION

1. On May 25, 1787, 55 delegates from every state except Rhode Island met in Philadelphia. The delegates quickly resolved to abandon the Articles of Confederation and create a new government.

2. During about 4 months of intense negotiations, the delegates seized control of America's destiny. They skillfully resolved contentious issues by reaching compromises that distinguished the possible from the impossible.

3. The Great Compromise resolved a dispute between the large states, led by Virginia, and the small states, led by New Jersey. The compromise created a bicameral, or two-house, Congress. Members of the House of Representatives would be apportioned on the basis of population, while each state would be allotted two seats in the Senate.

4. The words "slave" and "slavery" do not appear in the original Constitution. However, the Framers did indirectly recognize slavery in the Three-Fifths Compromise. Under the terms of this agreement, each slave counted as three-fifths of a person for purposes of determining a state's level of taxation and representation. This increased the congressional representation of the slave states and also gave them a greater voice in the Electoral College.

5. The Framers' decision to allow the importation of slaves to continue until 1808 also indirectly recognized the existence of slavery.

THE DEBATE OVER RATIFICATION

1. The Constitution would not go into effect until it was ratified by at least nine of the thirteen states.

2. A heated debate erupted between Federalists, who supported the Constitution, and Anti-Federalists, who opposed it.

3. The Anti-Federalists drew their primary support from small farmers and rural areas. They argued that the proposed Constitution lacked a Bill of Rights and that the new national government would dominate the states and threaten individual liberties.

4. The Federalists drew their primary support from large landowners, wealthy merchants, and urban areas. They argued that the proposed Constitution

would create a federal government with enough power to promote the general welfare and ensure domestic tranquility.

5. Written by James Madison, Alexander Hamilton, and John Jay, the *Federalist Papers* clearly articulated the Constitution's key principles.

6. The Federalists ensured the ratification of the Constitution by promising the addition of a Bill of Rights that would enumerate individual rights and explicitly restrict the powers of the federal government.

THE CONSTITUTION

1. The Constitution rectified flaws in the Articles of Confederation by granting the federal government the power to tax, coin money, regulate interstate commerce, and raise an army.

2. The Constitution created a federal system by granting specific powers to the national government while reserving other powers to the states.

3. The House of Representatives gave people a direct voice in the new government. However, the electoral college and the selection of senators by state legislatures expressed the Founders' desire to curb popular passions.

4. Charles Beard contended that wealthy white men wrote the Constitution as an economic document designed to protect private property. For example, the Three-Fifths Compromise was intended to protect the economic interests of slaveholders.

THE NEW REPUBLIC

1. George Washington commanded unmatched prestige and respect. His administration created institutions and precedents that put the principles of the Constitution into practice.

2. Alexander Hamilton served as America's first Secretary of the Treasury. At Washington's request, he submitted a series of far-reaching economic proposals. Hamilton's plans included funding the national debt at face value, assuming state debts, imposing tariffs on imported goods, and chartering a national bank.

3. Hamilton's proposal to charter a national bank triggered America's first debate on whether the Constitution should be interpreted strictly or loosely. Jefferson favored a "strict" interpretation by forcefully arguing that what the Constitution does not permit it forbids. Hamilton countered by favoring a "loose" interpretation arguing that what the Constitution does not forbid it permits.

4. Hamilton's arguments prevailed, and Washington signed the bank bill into law, thus chartering the First National Bank of the United States.

5. Political parties are not mentioned in the Constitution. However, parties began to coalesce around the economic policies and political views of Alexander Hamilton and Thomas Jefferson. The Federalist Party supported Hamilton's programs while opponents led by Jefferson founded the Democratic-Republican party.

6. The emergence of the Federalists and the Democratic-Republicans inaugurated America's two-party system. Historians divide American political history into party eras. The first party era began with the election of John Adams in 1796.

7. George Washington's Farewell Address encouraged national unity. He cautioned against political factions and warned about the danger of entering into permanent alliances with European powers.

LOOKING IN-DEPTH
THE CONSEQUENCES OF THE FRENCH AND INDIAN WAR

Great Britain emerged from the French and Indian War as the dominant power in North America. In Massachusetts, the Reverend Thomas Barnard praised Britain's "patriot-sovereign, wise counsellors, brave commanders and successful armies." He looked forward to an enduring new era of peace and prosperity. Reverend Barnwell would have been shocked to know that his prediction of a lasting era of peace and loyalty would prove to be completely wrong. Instead, the colonies and Britain entered a period of increasing tensions and disloyalty that culminated in the outbreak of the Revolutionary War in 1776.

Like most of his contemporaries, Reverend Barnard failed to perceive that the French and Indian War dramatically altered the relationship between Great Britain and her thirteen American colonies. The Peace of Paris of 1763 gave Britain title to Canada and all the French lands east of the Mississippi River. However, the new territories led to greater administrative costs and increased tensions with unruly Native American tribes. The British government therefore decided to send an armed force of 10,000 troops to North America to defend against "Indian" troubles and the threat posed by 9,000 restive French-Canadian Catholics.

The French and Indian War doubled Britain's national debt from 72 million pounds to 130 million pounds. Lord Grenville proposed to raise revenue by enforcing the long-neglected Navigation Acts and by imposing revenue taxes. Enacted in 1765, the Stamp Act ignited an increasingly bitter ideological debate about the relationship between Parliament and the colonial legislatures. The argument about taxes intensified the colonial commitment to a republican government based upon the consent of the governed.

So why should you remember the consequences of the French and Indian War? Test writers often ask students to identify maps depicting North America before and after the French and Indian War. It is also important to remember that the war set in motion a series of changes that fundamentally altered political, economic, and ideological relations between Britain and the American colonies.

THE FRENCH ALLIANCE

Why did the United States defeat Great Britain in the Revolutionary War? When I was in high school, we learned that American patriots were inspired by democratic ideas, guided by Washington's pivotal decisions, and helped by Britain's blundering generals. Although this is the traditional textbook answer, it is not how APUSH test writers view the Revolutionary War. While the APUSH test development committee members recognize the role of traditional factors, they place a much greater emphasis upon the importance of the French Alliance.

It is important to remember that France's king Louis XVI was not sympathetic to republican values. Instead, French leaders were motivated by a desire to avenge their humiliating loss to Great Britain in the Seven Years' War.

At first, the cautious French secretly provided vital military supplies and money to the colonies. The American victory at Saratoga convinced France that America had the ability to defeat Great Britain. France then recognized the United States on February 6, 1778.

The French Alliance prevented any chance of an Anglo-American reconciliation. French military and financial aid played a decisive role in enabling America to win the Revolutionary War. For example, the French fleet prevented the British from rescuing Cornwallis at Yorktown. Cornwallis then surrendered to an evenly divided American-French army of 16,000 men.

So why should you remember the French Alliance? The French Alliance is an exception to the rule that APUSH exams rarely ask questions about military history. It is important to remember that France negotiated a treaty of alliance with the United States following the British defeat at Saratoga. French military and financial assistance played an indispensable role in the American victory in the Revolutionary War.

SHAYS'S REBELLION, 1787

In autumn 1786 farmers in western Massachusetts faced a familiar problem: A distant government was imposing heavy taxes on its citizens, forcing many of them into debt. Only this time, the distant government was not Parliament in London but the state legislature in Boston.

Just a few years after the Revolutionary War, angry Massachusetts farmers were losing their farms because they could not repay their debts to eastern merchants and bankers in hard currency. Desperate farmers demanded that the state legislature halt farm foreclosures, lower property taxes, print paper money, and end imprisonment for debt.

Led by Daniel Shays, a 39 year-old former captain in the Continental Army, armed farmers closed a courthouse where creditors were suing to foreclose farm mortgages. In January, 1787, hastily-mustered state troops crushed the rebellion. Shays then fled to Vermont and was later pardoned.

So why should you remember Shays's Rebellion? Shays's Rebellion frightened conservative leaders who feared that an unchecked democratic mob would destroy orderly government. By exposing the weaknesses of the Articles of the Confederation, Shays's Rebellion provided persuasive arguments for Madison, Hamilton, Washington, and other leaders pushing for a new Constitutional Convention. To these men, Shays's Rebellion underscored the need to create a stronger national government. Although Daniel Shays was not present at the Constitutional Convention, he should nonetheless be considered an influential figure in the steps leading to the adoption of the Constitution.

THE *FEDERALIST PAPERS*, 1787

The Constitution did not go into effect once the Constitutional Convention in Philadelphia was over. It had to be ratified by at least 9 of the 13 states.

Throughout the states, a fierce battle erupted between the Federalists, who supported the Constitution, and the Anti-Federalists, who opposed it. Newspapers were filled with letters and articles praising or condemning the document.

James Madison, Alexander Hamilton, and John Jay wrote a series of 85 essays now known as the *Federalist Papers*. The essays began to appear in late October 1787 in New York newspapers as part of the ratification debate in that closely contested state. The *Federalist Papers* defended the Constitution point by point. In addition, they represented an important statement of political philosophy. The Federalists ultimately won an uphill battle in New York by a vote of 30 to 27.

So why should you remember the *Federalist Papers*? When the *Federalist Papers* were written, most political theorists believed that a republican form of government could only succeed in small countries. The *Federalist Papers* challenged conventional wisdom by asserting that a large republic actually offered the best protection of minority rights. It is also important to remember that in "Federalist No 10" Madison argued that political factions are undesirable but inevitable. He believed that in a large republic "so many different groups and viewpoints would be included in Congress that tyranny by the majority would be impossible."

THE ALIEN AND SEDITION ACTS, 1798

Have you ever had a plan that produced the opposite consequences of what you expected? Well, that is what happened to the Federalists in 1798. At that time, America seemed to be on the brink of declaring war on France. The Federalists decided that public anger at France would provide a perfect opportunity to strike a decisive blow at their political opponents the Democratic-Republicans.

In 1798 the Federalist-controlled Congress passes a series of acts known as the Alien and Sedition Acts. The Naturalization Act raised the residency requirement for US citizens from 5 to 14 years. Outraged Democratic-Republicans insisted that the act's real purpose was to prevent immigrants from voting for their party. The Sedition Act mandated heavy fines and imprisonment for all those found guilty of writing, publishing, and speaking against the federal government. The law's true intent was to repress the outspoken Republican press, long a thorn in the side of the Federalist Party.

The Alien and Sedition Acts proved to be both unnecessary and ineffective. Instead of suppressing the Democratic-Republicans, the acts enraged Jefferson and his followers. Convinced that the acts were designed to destroy their party, the Democratic-Republicans rallied behind Jefferson and won the presidency in 1800. The Sedition Acts expired in 1801 and Congress repealed the Naturalization Act in 1802.

So why should you remember the Alien and Sedition Acts? The acts prompted Jefferson and Madison to write a series of resolutions that were approved by the Kentucky and Virginia legislatures. As expected, the resolutions denounced the Alien and Sedition Acts as "alarming infractions" of Constitutional rights. However, the Kentucky and Virginia Resolutions went one step further by formulating a states' rights doctrine asserting that the Constitution arose as a compact among sovereign states. According to Jefferson and Madison, the states therefore retained the power to challenge and, if necessary, nullify federal laws. The Kentucky and Virginia Resolutions thus advanced arguments that John C. Calhoun would later adopt during the nullification crisis of the 1830s.

CHAPTER 4
PERIOD 4
1800 – 1848

TIMELINE

1800   Election of Thomas Jefferson

1800   Second Great Awakening begins

1803   Louisiana Purchase

1803   *Marbury v. Madison*

1820   Missouri Compromise

1823   Monroe Doctrine

1825   Opening of the Erie Canal

1828   Election of Andrew Jackson

1831   William Lloyd Garrison publishes The Liberator

1838   Trail of Tears

1844   First telegraphic message

1845   Beginning of Irish immigration

1848   Seneca Falls Convention

CREATING A NEW NATION, 1800 – 1816

1. The election of 1800 is often called "The Revolution of 1800" because it marked a peaceful transfer of political power from the Federalists, led by John Adams, to the Democratic-Republicans, led by Thomas Jefferson. The election signaled the end of the Federalist Era.

2. Jefferson urged Congress to repeal the Alien and Sedition Acts. He successfully argued that freedom of speech is essential to a healthy republic.

3. Napoleon's unexpected offer to sell the entire Louisiana Territory confronted Jefferson with a dilemma. As a strict constructionist he worried that the

Constitution does not give Congress the power to purchase new territory. Despite his reservations, Jefferson recognized he had to act quickly. Congress promptly passed the treaty and Jefferson signed it.

4. The Louisiana Territory doubled the size of the United States. Jefferson optimistically believed the purchase would promote a broad distribution of property ownership that would enable America to become an "Empire of Liberty."

5. Chief Justice John Marshall believed he could best serve America by rendering judicial decisions that supported a strong central government and promoted business enterprise.

6. The Marshall Court established the principle of JUDICIAL REVIEW in *Marbury v. Madison*. Judicial review gave the Supreme Court the power to strike down a Congressional action found to violate a provision of the Constitution.

7. The War of 1812 promoted an increase in domestic manufacturing, intensified a spirit of national unity, caused the final demise of the Federalist Party, and catapulted Andrew Jackson into a national hero.

THE ERA OF GOOD FEELINGS, 1816 – 1824

1. James Monroe easily defeated his Federalist opponents in the 1816 presidential election. One Boston newspaper captured the optimistic spirit of the time when it proclaimed that Monroe's election marked the beginning of a period of national unity it named "The Era of Good Feelings."

2. Jefferson lived to see that purchasing and exploring the Louisiana Territory proved to be more difficult than organizing and governing it. In 1819, the territory of Missouri applied for statehood as a slave state.

3. At that time the Senate was evenly divided between 11 free states and 11 slave states. House Speaker Henry Clay proposed a compromise designed to preserve the balance in Senate by admitting Missouri as a slave state and Maine as a free state.

4. In addition, the compromise restricted slavery above Missouri's southern border, thereby creating slave and non-slave regions. The North viewed this agreement as a "sacred pact" that should never be broken.

5. The Missouri Compromise temporarily defused the political crisis over the expansion of slavery into the western territories. However, the controversy hardened the South's defense of slavery as a positive good, essential to the region's economy and way of life.

6. Sponsored by Henry Clay, the American system supported a national bank to promote economic stability, a tariff to raise revenue and protect American industries, and the construction of a network of canals and roads to unite the country.

7. Clay's American System strongly resembled Hamilton's economic policies. Both programs favored a strong federal government to promote commerce and economic growth.

8. In his final message to Congress on December 2, 1823, President Monroe announced a new American policy that later became known as the Monroe Doctrine. Issued as a unilateral declaration of principles, the Monroe Doctrine declared that republican governments in the Americas were different and separate from the monarchical systems in Europe. As the protector of republican institutions, the United States would not tolerate the creation of new European colonies in the Western Hemisphere.

9. Monroe's declaration underscored America's growing self-confidence in the Era of Good Feelings. First called the Monroe Doctrine in 1852, the principles Monroe proclaimed became the cornerstone of American foreign policy in the Western Hemisphere.

THE MARKET REVOLUTION IN COMMERCE AND PRODUCTION

1. During the Era of Good Feelings, most Americans produced goods for local markets. However, between 1820 and 1860, canals, steamboats, and railroads created a Market Revolution by enlarging markets and fostering regional interdependence.

2. Steamboats carried bulky farm products such as wheat, corn, and flour far more cheaply than covered wagons. By the 1840s, steamboats opened the Ohio and Mississippi river valleys to two-way traffic.

3. The Erie Canal created an all-water route that cut travel time from New York City to Buffalo from 20 days to six and reduced the cost of moving a ton of freight between these two cities from $100.00 to $5.00. The Erie Canal sparked the rapid growth of Buffalo while helping transform New York City into America's greatest commercial center.

4. Railroads connected cities, encouraged settlement, and reduced the cost of transporting goods. The number of miles of railroad track soared from just 13 when the Baltimore and Ohio opened in 1829 to 30,626 in 1860.

5. Innovations including textile machinery, steam engines, the telegraph, and agricultural innovations such as the steel plow and mechanical

reaper increased the efficiency of production methods. The creation of profitable regional and interregional markets led to an American system of manufacturing that utilized machines with interchangeable parts to mass produce standardized low-cost goods.

6. The Market Revolution had a significant impact on economic life in the Northeast. It created close commercial ties with the Old Northwest, hastened the shift from hand-made to machine-made goods, and accelerated a transition to a wage-based economy.

7. The Market Revolution also had a significant impact on economic life in the Midwest. It accelerated the migration of settlers into the region, transformed Chicago into an important transportation hub, and closely linked the economies of the Midwest and the Northeast.

8. The South failed to keep up with the pace of industrialization and urbanization in the Northeast and Midwest. A "Cotton Kingdom" based upon slave labor extended across the Deep South. Led by a wealthy group of planters, the South adopted a distinctive regional identity.

THE CULT OF DOMESTICITY

1. Prior to the Market Revolution, men and women worked together as an economic team on small family farms. However, as the Market Revolution gained momentum, it encouraged a division of labor between two separate spheres – work and home.

2. "True Men" were expected to earn success in the ruthlessly competitive world of business and politics. In contrast, "True Women" were expected to devote their energies to creating a stable and peaceful home.

3. The earlier ideal of republican motherhood gradually evolved into a new cultural model known as the CULT OF DOMESTICITY. This set of beliefs idealized women in their roles as wives and mothers. As a nurturing mother and a faithful spouse, the wife created a home that was a "haven in a heartless world." The home thus became a refuge, and the wife became what one popular women's magazine called "the light of the house."

4. The cult of domesticity embodied a cultural ideal that best applied to upper- and middle-class families who could afford to maintain separate spheres for their work and home lives. However, a wide gap separated these privileged groups from the mill women working in factories, the frontier women working on isolated farms, and the enslaved African women working on cotton plantations.

5. Some women in New England supplemented their household income by working in textile mills. The Lowell mill girls comprised America's first female labor force. The cult of domesticity had little impact on their lives. They worked long hours and lived in tightly regulated dormitories.

THE RISE OF MASS DEMOCRACY

1. The Framers of the United States Constitution believed voting rights should be restricted to a natural aristocracy of propertied gentlemen. They limited the franchise to prosperous merchants and planters who had a stake in the government. The First Party System provided stability by allowing peaceful transfers of power from one set of elite leaders to another.

2. During the 1820s, state legislatures eliminated most property qualifications, enabling a growing number of white males to vote. The expanded electorate had a dramatic effect upon the rise of new political parties and the emergence of new styles of political campaigning.

3. Led by Martin Van Buren, Jackson's supporters shrewdly launched a new style of campaigning that included parades, mass rallies, leaflets, banners, barbecues, and, of course, generous quantities of hard cider.

4. The expanded democracy still excluded enslaved Africans, free Black people, women, and Native Americans.

THE AGE OF JACKSON

1. Andrew Jackson's supporters praised him as a common man who represented the interests of the people. A wave of enthusiastic popular support swept "Old Hickory" into the White House.

2. The Jacksonians enthusiastically supported the expansion of white male suffrage. During the Jackson administration, nominating conventions replaced legislative caucuses.

3. As champions of the common man, the Jacksonians despised the privileges of the Eastern elite. Jackson vetoed a bill that would have rechartered the Second Bank of the United States. He denounced the bank as a vehicle used by the rich and powerful to bend the acts of government to their selfish interests.

4. Jackson's war against the bank played a key role in the creation of the new two-party system. Now known as Democrats, Jackson's party opposed the bank and supported states' rights. Led by Henry Clay, the Whigs supported the bank and Clay's American System of internal improvements.

5. Jackson supported the Indian Removal Act, providing for the forced removal of eastern tribes to the newly established Indian Territory in what is now Oklahoma. In 1838, federal troops began a forced evacuation of about 17,000 Cherokees from their tribal lands. About one-fourth died from disease and exhaustion on the 800-mile route that became known as the Trail of Tears.

A NEW NATIONAL CULTURE

1. TRANSCENDENTALISM was a philosophical and literary movement that stressed the importance of intuition, nonconformity, and the belief that truth could be found in nature. Ralph Waldo Emerson, Henry David Thoreau, and Margaret Fuller were the leading transcendentalists.

2. A group of artists known as the Hudson River School applied the transcendentalist reverence to nature to art. Hudson River School artists painted landscapes that idealized the beauty of the American countryside.

3. Romantic poets also looked to nature for insights about truth and beauty. For example, Walt Whitman's famous volume of poems, *Leaves of Grass*, rejected reason while emphasizing feeling and emotion. In his poem, "When I Heard the Learn'd Astronomer," Whitman argued that a Romantic perspective can yield deeper insights about truth and beauty than a scientific perspective.

4. Idealists founded over 100 utopian communities, where they tried new ways of organizing work and daily life. Utopian communities rejected competitive business practices, favored communal living arrangements, opposed strict moral rules, and believed in sharing their wealth.

THE SECOND GREAT AWAKENING

1. The SECOND GREAT AWAKENING was a wave of religious fervor that swept across America between 1800 and 1830. Thousands of people attended emotionally charged camp meetings featuring appeals to faith and conversion by charismatic preachers.

2. Intense religious revivals were especially widespread in central and western New York. This region became known as the "Burned-Over District" because of the particularly enthusiastic revivals that crisscrossed the area.

3. The Burned-Over District was the birthplace of the Church of Jesus Christ of Latter-Day Saints, or Mormons. Founded in the 1820s by Joseph Smith, Mormonism attracted a number of loyal followers. In 1847, Brigham Young

led more than 2,000 Mormons on an arduous journey to the shores of the Great Salt Lake in Utah.

4. Puritan ministers taught that God controlled each individual's destiny. In contrast, Charles Grandison Finney delivered inspiring sermons stressing that Christians are not doomed by original sin. Instead, he emphasized humanity's inherent goodness and each individual's potential for self-improvement.

5. Charles Grandison Finney and other Second Great Awakening preachers stressed that each individual was a "moral free agent" who could improve his or her life.

AN AGE OF REFORM

1. It was a short step from the Second Great Awakening's emphasis upon spiritual progress to a belief in the possibility of social progress. The Second Great Awakening inspired a commitment to PERFECTIONISM – faith in the human ability to build a just society.

2. The close link between religion and reform awakened America to the evils of slavery. For example, the call for moral reform influenced William Lloyd Garrison's demand for the immediate emancipation of all enslaved people.

3. Middle-class women played an especially important role in the Second Great Awakening. They boosted church membership and also spearheaded a number of reform movements. For example, Dorothea Dix urged more humane treatment for the mentally ill. A compelling moral purpose led many women to join Garrison's American Anti-Slavery Society.

4. Elizabeth Cady Stanton and Lucretia Mott concluded that women and slaves both shared a history of injustice. In 1848, they issued a public call for a convention in Seneca Falls, New York to discuss women's rights.

5. The Seneca Falls Convention issued a "Declaration of Sentiments and Resolutions" calling for greater access to education, a change in divorce and child custody rights, and the extension of suffrage to women.

6. The ideas advanced by the Seneca Falls Convention differed from the ideas of republican motherhood. Under republican motherhood, women exercised an indirect political role through their roles as mothers and educators of male citizens. In contrast, women at the Seneca Falls Convention claimed a direct role in American political life.

7. The Seneca Falls Convention marked the beginning of the women's rights movement in the United States. The resolutions passed at Seneca Falls formed the agenda for what historians now call first-wave feminism.

SLAVERY AND THE OLD SOUTH

1. In 1790, the once vibrant Southern economy began to stagnate as tobacco lost its value as a cash crop. However, the invention of the cotton gin in 1793 revolutionized the Southern economy and the lives of enslaved Africans.

2. The cotton gin transformed cotton into America's most valuable cash crop. By 1860, a vast cotton belt stretched from South Carolina to the Mississippi River Valley. Known as the Deep South, this region produced three-fourths of the world's supply of cotton. Proud Southern planters confidently boasted, "Cotton is King."

3. Cotton irrevocably changed the South's attitude toward slavery. Prior to the invention of the cotton gin, many thoughtful Southerners referred to slavery as a "necessary evil" inherited from their colonial past. However, during the 1820s and 1830s, slaveholders worked out a systematic proslavery argument to justify their "peculiar institution" as a "positive good." As the South became committed to a cotton economy, the region also became committed to slavery.

4. The presence of unpaid slave labor discouraged European immigrants from settling in the South. As the South devoted more and more resources to slave labor and cotton, the region failed to fully participate in the transportation revolution transforming the rest of America's economy.

5. A small but powerful group of planters owned more than half of the South's slaves. The majority of white families in the antebellum South were independent yeoman farmers who owned few, if any, slaves.

6. Congress ended the slave trade in 1808. As a result, planters could no longer import slaves from Africa or the West Indies. Instead, they bought slaves from planters in Virginia and Maryland. Between 1810 and 1860, over two million slaves endured a forced migration from the Chesapeake area to the slaveholding states in the Deep South.

7. The spread of cotton plantations to the Deep South uprooted countless enslaved Africans. Despite this disruption, slaves maintained strong kinship networks while creating a separate African American culture. Religion played a particularly important role. For example, spiritual songs enabled slaves to express their sorrows, joys, and hopes for a better life.

LOOKING IN-DEPTH
THE LOUISIANA PURCHASE, 1803

Do the ends justify the means? Napoleon Bonaparte forced Thomas Jefferson to confront this age-old question when he unexpectedly offered to sell the entire Louisiana Territory to the United States.

It is important to remember that Jefferson advocated a strict interpretation of the Constitution. In his debate with Hamilton over the National Bank Jefferson insisted that what the Constitution does not permit it forbids. Jefferson recognized that the Constitution did not expressly grant the President the power to acquire foreign territory. So how could Jefferson approve Napoleon's offer to sell the entire Louisiana Territory?

A combination of pragmatic benefits and an idealistic dream forced Jefferson to set aside his constitutional objections. The Louisiana Purchase would enable America to control the vital port of New Orleans. In addition, the purchase would double the size of the United States, giving the country almost limitless room for expansion. The vast new territories would help fulfill Jefferson's vision of enabling America to become an agrarian republic and thus an Empire of Liberty. Fearing that the always capricious Napoleon might change his mind, Jefferson relented and the Senate overwhelmingly approved the Louisiana Purchase.

So why should you remember the Louisiana Purchase? The Louisiana Purchase ended the French threat to New Orleans and doubled the size of the United States. It set a precedent for acquiring foreign territory and people by treaty. However, the land acquired in the Louisiana Purchase soon sparked a sectional dispute over the spread of slavery into the new western territories.

MARBURY V. MADISON, 1803

Have you ever faced a seemingly hopeless situation? Most people have. But the real question is, were you able to snatch victory from the jaws of what appeared to be certain defeat? John Marshall, the Chief Justice of the Supreme Court, accomplished this feat in a landmark decision in the case of *Marbury v. Madison*. Let me explain:

As you know, Jefferson and the Democratic-Republicans swept to victory in the election of 1800. The Federalists feared that Jefferson's victory placed their effort to create a strong federal government in grave jeopardy. In his final days in office, Adams tried to turn the judicial branch into a last bastion of Federalist power. First, he appointed John Marshall as the new Chief Justice of the Supreme Court. Marshall was a staunch Federalist, committed to strengthening the power of the federal government. Then, on his last day in office, Adams appointed a number of so-called Federalist "midnight judges."

As fate would have it, the Adams Administration failed to properly deliver all the commissions of the midnight justices. President Jefferson therefore refused to honor Adams's appointments on the grounds that the paperwork had not been delivered to the proper offices before the change of administration had taken place. William Marbury, an ardent Federalist and successful financier, sued Jefferson's Secretary of State, James Madison, asking the Supreme Court to issue a writ of mandamus forcing Madison to deliver his commission.

Chief Justice Marshall now faced a difficult decision. On the one hand, Marshall wanted the Supreme Court to play a strong role as the guardian of the Constitution. On the other hand, Marshall knew that the Jefferson administration might not enforce a writ to deliver the commission to Marbury. Marshall solved his dilemma by dismissing Marbury's suit, thus avoiding a direct confrontation with Jefferson. But he cleverly snatched victory from the jaws of defeat by asserting that the part of the Judiciary Act of 1789 on which Marbury tried to base his claim was unconstitutional.

So why should you remember the Supreme Court decision in *Marbury v. Madison*? APUSH test writers will not expect you to recall the details of this complex case. But they will expect you to know that *Marbury v. Madison* established the principle of judicial review, the authority of the Supreme Court to determine the constitutionality of congressional acts. Judicial review thus gave the Supreme Court the power to make definitive rulings on the meaning of the Constitution.

THE MONROE DOCTRINE, 1823

On December 2, 1823, President James Monroe stood before the Congress of the United States to read his annual message. Most of the president's speech focused on domestic matters and are now forgotten. However, Monroe's relatively short pronouncement on foreign affairs was destined to take on historic importance as the basis of a major declaration of American foreign policy. "The American Continents," Monroe announced, "are henceforth not to be considered as subjects for further colonization by a European power."

What prompted Monroe's bold and unexpected declaration? Between 1803 and 1822, Spain lost almost all of its entire New World empire as Chile, Peru, Columbia, and Mexico all successfully waged wars of liberation. President Monroe and Secretary of State John Quincy Adams feared that France might use force to help Spain overthrow the new American republics.

Monroe responded to the perceived threat by issuing a unilateral declaration warning the European powers that the American continent was no longer open to European colonization. Monroe also declared that the republican governments in the Americas were different from the monarchical governments in Europe. The United States would therefore regard European interference in the political affairs of independent New World nations as hostile behavior.

Monroe's bold statement of principles received little attention at the time. The European powers refrained from interfering in the New World because of the power of British warships, not the eloquence of Monroe's words.

So why should you remember the Monroe Doctrine? Monroe's principles were not forgotten. First called the Monroe Doctrine in 1852, they became the cornerstone of American foreign policy in the Western Hemisphere. In December, 1904, President Theodore Roosevelt added a corollary to the Monroe Doctrine in which he stated that the United States would not interfere with Latin American nations that conducted their affairs with decency. However, if they failed to live up to this standard, the United States would intervene and exercise an international police power.

THE ERIE CANAL, 1825

In 1817 farmers in the Old Northwest harvested abundant crops of wheat, millet, apples, and potatoes while also exploiting the region's lumber and fur resources. However, the Appalachian Mountains blocked their access to consumers in East Coast cities. As a result, they were forced to send their bulky products to market by way of the Ohio and Mississippi Rivers to New Orleans and then transfer the cargo to ocean vessels that could reach East Coast ports.

The governor of New York, DeWitt Clinton, had a bold but risky idea to eliminate this circuitous trade route. Clinton proposed to build a 363-mile canal that would connect Buffalo, on Lake Erie, with Albany, on the Hudson River. Special canal packets could then easily glide down the Hudson River to New York City.

Critics promptly labelled the proposed Erie Canal "DeWitt's Ditch." They pointed out that the longest canal in America extended only 28 miles. The Erie Canal would require construction crews to dig a 40-foot wide channel through wilderness terrain while engineers designed a complex system of locks and aqueducts.

Clinton ignored his critics and pushed ahead. Within just 8 years, his team of builders accomplished the impossible. On October 26, 1825, Governor Clinton boarded a brightly decorated canal boat in Buffalo, New York. Named the *Seneca Chief*, the boat glided down the just-opened Erie Canal and headed east to Albany. The *Seneca Chief* completed the 363-mile trip in just 5 days. The ship then passed into the Hudson River and headed south to New York City. The climax of the 9-day journey occurred at the entrance to New York harbor. As thousands of spectators cheered, Governor Clinton triumphantly poured a keg of fresh water from Lake Erie into the salt water of the Atlantic Ocean. This "Wedding of the Waters" symbolized the joining of the inland Great Lakes with the Atlantic Ocean.

So why should you remember the Erie Canal? The canal proved to be an enormous success with far-reaching consequences. It tightened economic bonds between Northern coastal cities and the farmlands in the Old Northwest. As the volume of trade between the two regions increased, New York City quickly emerged as America's greatest commercial center. And finally, the Erie Canal inspired a mania for building canals that lasted throughout the 1830s. The Erie Canal thus played a key role in the rapid growth of the market revolution.

THE SENECA FALLS CONVENTION, 1848

In June 1840, Elizabeth Cady Stanton, Lucretia Mott, and their husbands travelled to London to attend the World Anti-Slavery Convention. Filled with idealism, Stanton and Mott eagerly looked forward to sharing their ideas with the other delegates. However, Stanton and Mott soon discovered that the male delegates voted to relegate women to an area behind a curtain. Cordoned off like second-class citizens, the women could only listen to the convention proceedings. Outraged by this blatant discrimination, Stanton and Mott resolved to organize a women's rights convention when they returned to America.

Eight years passed before Stanton and Mott were able to turn their pledge into a reality. In July 1848, they placed a notice in the *Seneca County Courier* in which they called upon women and men to attend "a convention to discuss the social, civil, and religious condition and rights of women." Inspired by the notice, about 300 women and men gathered at the Wesleyan Chapel in Seneca Falls, New York.

The women delegates had a number of legitimate grievances. At that time, men dominated the public sphere by voting and participating in politics. In contrast, the prevailing ideal of domesticity assigned women to a domestic sphere where they cooked, cleaned, and raised children. Stanton condemned "disgraceful laws" giving men the legal power to control women's wages, property, and children.

At that time women rarely spoke in public. Stanton nonetheless read a Declaration of Sentiments and Resolutions. Inspired by the Declaration of Independence, the document began by declaring, "We hold these truths to be self-evident; that all men and women are created equal." The convention delegates unanimously approved resolutions calling for greater divorce and child custody rights, equal opportunities in education, and a woman's right to retain property after marriage.

The list of resolutions also included a controversial demand for "the sacred right to the elective franchise." This unprecedented demand shocked and divided the convention delegates. Even Stanton's husband refused to support women's suffrage. However, the suffrage resolution narrowly passed when the renowned abolitionist leader Frederick Douglass persuaded delegates that the right to vote is a fundamental principle of equality.

So why should you remember the Seneca Falls Convention? The historic meeting marked the beginning of the women's rights movement in the United States. The demands in the Declaration of Sentiments and Resolutions formed the movement's agenda until the passage of the Nineteenth Amendment granting women the right to vote.

CHAPTER 5
PERIOD 5
1844 – 1877

TIMELINE

1844   Polk elected president

1846   Mexican-American War

1846   Wilmot Proviso

1848   Treaty of Guadalupe Hidalgo

1848   Gold discovered in California

1850   Compromise of 1850

1852   Harriet Beecher Stowe published *Uncle Tom's Cabin*

1854   Kansas-Nebraska Act

1854   Know-Nothing Party established

1857   Dred Scott decision

1858   Lincoln-Douglas debates

1860   Lincoln elected president

1861   Fort Sumter fired on

1863   Lincoln issues the Emancipation Proclamation

1865   Lee surrenders to Grant

1865   Lincoln assassinated

1865   Thirteenth Amendment ends slavery

1866   Black Codes

1868   Fourteenth Amendment ratified

1868   Impeachment and trial of President Johnson

1870   Fifteenth Amendment

1877   Compromise of 1877 ends Reconstruction

MANIFEST DESTINY

1. The Missouri Compromise seemingly settled the status of slavery in the western territories. American leaders carefully avoided policies that would reopen sectional tensions over the future of slavery.

2. The American public enthusiastically supported western expansion. Settlers hoped to discover veins of gold and silver, obtain fertile land for farms, and seek safe havens where they could freely practice their religion.

3. John O'Sullivan coined the term MANIFEST DESTINY in 1845. The phrase successfully captured the linkage between western expansion and America's self-proclaimed mission to spread the blessings of liberty and progress across the continent.

4. Territorial expansion inevitably placed slavery at the center of American politics. During the 1840s and 1850s, American leaders proved unable to find a satisfactory way to avoid the gathering storm over slavery.

THE MEXICAN–AMERICAN WAR

1. The issue of territorial expansion dominated the 1844 presidential election. As the campaign began, Texas still remained independent and California still belonged to Mexico.

2. The Democratic presidential nominee James K. Polk narrowly defeated the Whig candidate Henry Clay. Polk's campaign promised to turn the idea of Manifest Destiny into a geographic reality.

3. Shortly after the election, California approved a resolution annexing Texas as the nation's 28th state. The annexation of Texas outraged Mexico and led to the outbreak of the Mexican-American War.

4. Whigs criticized Manifest Destiny as an excuse for justifying the war with Mexico. New England abolitionists forcefully argued that the slogan "extend the area of freedom" really meant extending the institution of slavery.

5. American forces defeated Mexico in a short war. By the terms of the Treaty of Guadalupe Hidalgo, Mexico gave up all claims to Texas above the Rio Grande River and ceded California and New Mexico to the United States. Manifest Destiny thus transformed the United States into a transcontinental republic.

THE WILMOT PROVISO

1. The Mexican-American War did not give rise to a period of national harmony. The postwar spirit of nationalism quickly faded as sectional struggles over the territorial expansion of slavery began to dominate American political life.

2. Known as the Mexican Cession, the vast lands gained in the Treaty of Guadalupe Hidalgo led to heated controversies over whether to allow slavery in the newly acquired territories.

3. On August 8, 1846, David Wilmot, a first-term congressman from Pennsylvania, attached an amendment, or proviso, to a military appropriations bill. The Wilmot Proviso banned slavery from all the territories acquired from Mexico. Wilmot pointed out that the Northwest Ordinance of 1787 and the Missouri Compromise provided precedents for the right of Congress to restrict slavery in the new territories.

4. Wilmot and his supporters defended the proviso as a necessary measure to insure the "rights of white freemen" to live and work in the new territories without the unfair disadvantage of competing with slave labor. "Free soil" would guarantee liberty, equal competition, social mobility, and a worker's "right to rise."

5. The House of Representatives passed the Wilmot Proviso. However, the South successfully blocked the legislation in the Senate. Although the Wilmot Proviso did not become law, it did become a rally point for an antislavery coalition that formed the Free Soil Party.

THE COMPROMISE OF 1850

1. On January 24, 1848, James Marshall discovered gold along the south fork of the American River east of San Francisco. As news of Marshall's discovery spread across the country, a great human wave of fortune hunters rushed to California. During 1849, over 80,000 "forty-niners" reached the once thinly populated territory. The new Californians promptly drew up a constitution asking Congress to admit them into the Union as a free state.

2. California's petition for statehood renewed the still unresolved debate over the spread of slavery into the territories won in the Mexican War. In 1850, the Union included 15 free states and 15 slave states.

3. The balance of power in the Senate was not the only issue dividing the North and the South. In 1850, Washington, D.C., served as a thriving and profitable center of the domestic slave trade. Groups of chained slaves often passed by the Capitol building and the White House. The sight of

human bondage deeply offended abolitionists who denounced the odious practice as a national disgrace.

4. Reaching an agreement between the North and South had been difficult in 1820. It proved to be even harder in 1850. Southern leaders feared that the North would use its growing strength to threaten slavery and reduce this proud region to the status of a permanent minority.

5. After long negotiations, Henry Clay, Stephen Douglas, and Daniel Webster reached the following agreements:

   • The immediate admission of California as a free state

   • The abolition of the domestic slave trade, but not slavery itself, in Washington, D.C.

   • The establishment of territorial governments in the rest of the Mexican Cession "without the adoption of any restriction or condition on the subject of slavery."

   • Monetary compensation to Texas for the withdrawal of its claims to portions of New Mexico.

   • The enactment of a strict new Fugitive Slave Law

6. Known as the Compromise of 1850, these agreements seemed to defuse the crisis and establish an uneasy sectional peace.

IMMIGRANTS AND NATIVISTS

1. During the 1830 and early 1840s, Anglo-Protestants, enslaved Africans, and Native Americans comprised America's most significant ethnic and racial groups. However, that began to change in 1845 when a blight swept across Ireland's farms and ruined the nation's entire potato crop. Faced with starvation and death, about 1.7 million Irish men, women, and children abandoned their homeland in a mass exodus to America.

2. The Irish immigrants poured into fast-growing port cities along the Northeast coast. Lacking jobs and financial resources, they performed menial and dangerous jobs. Irish men dug canals, laid railroad tracks, and unloaded cargo ships, while Irish women cleaned homes and toiled in New England textile mills.

3. The 1840s also witnessed the beginning of a massive wave of immigrants from Germany. A diverse group, the Germans included exiled political refugees, farmers disposed by industrial development, and Jews fleeing religious persecution. Unlike the Irish, the Germans settled in farms and in Midwestern cities such as Milwaukee, St. Louis, and Chicago.

4. Unwilling to compete with slave labor, very few Irish or German immigrants settled in the South.

5. The sudden flood of Irish immigrants added to tensions in the increasingly volatile mix of people living in the Northeast's booming cities. The Catholic Church's ornate ceremonies contrasted with the simple services in Protestant churches. At the same time, black-robed priests and nuns seemed strange and threatening.

6. Anti-Catholic and anti-immigrant passions sparked the formation of a nativist political party popularly known as the "Know-Nothings." The party platform forcefully declared, "Americas must rule America!"

7. The Know-Nothings achieved initial electoral success. However, the anti-Catholic fervor subsided as immigration declined and the country shifted its focus to the growing national debate over slavery.

THE GATHERING STORM

1. The Compromise of 1850 did not end the agitation over slavery. Designed to placate the South, the Fugitive Slave Act had the unintended consequence of inflaming Northern public opinion against slavery. The sight of professional slave hunters roaming across the Northern free states raised fears of a "slave power conspiracy."

2. The rising furor over the Fugitive Slave Act inspired Harriet Beecher Stowe to write *Uncle Tom's Cabin*. The novel proved to be a bestseller that intensified Northern opposition to slavery.

3. Both the Kansas and Nebraska territories were located in the part of the Louisiana Territory where the Missouri Compromise banned slavery.

4. Senator Stephen A. Douglas of Illinois reopened the issue of slavery in the territories by proposing to allow the people of Kansas and Nebraska to decide for themselves if their territories would enter the Union as free or slave states. Letting settlers in a given territory have the sole right to decide whether or not slavery would be permitted within their boundaries was known as POPULAR SOVEREIGNTY.

5. Douglas proposed a bill known as the Kansas-Nebraska Act to organize Kansas and Nebraska based upon the principle of popular sovereignty.

6. Congress passed the Kansas-Nebraska Act after a long and bitter debate. The legislation had several momentous consequences:

   • It effectively repealed the Missouri Compromise ban on the extension of slavery into the Louisiana Territory.

- It galvanized a spontaneous outpouring of popular opposition in the North that led to the formation of the Republican Party.

- It led to the demise of the Whig Party, thus ending the Second Party System.

- It split the Democratic Party into Northern and Southern wings.

7. The Dred Scott decision ruled that neither slaves nor free blacks were citizens in the political community created by the Constitution. This ruling struck down both the Northwest Ordinance and the Missouri Compromise. The decision sharpened sectional tensions by reinforcing the Southern view that the Constitution safeguarded the extension of slavery into the western territories.

THE ELECTION OF 1860 AND SECESSION

1. The 1860 Republican Party platform accepted slavery in the states where it existed. However, the Republicans opposed any further extension of slavery into any of the western territories. The Democrats were divided on this issue.

2. The Republican presidential candidate, Abraham Lincoln, won the 1860 presidential election by carrying only states in the North plus California and Oregon. Lincoln failed to win any of the border states or states in the South.

3. Lincoln's election prompted South Carolina and six other Deep South states to secede from the Union.

4. In a final desperate effort to save the Union, Senator John Crittenden of Kentucky proposed to restore the boundary line between free and slave states established by the Missouri Compromise of 1820.

5. Lincoln rejected the Crittenden Compromise because it violated the Republican Party's firm position against the further extension of slavery into the western territories.

6. Shortly after Lincoln took office, Confederate troops fired on Fort Sumter, leading to the secession of four additional Southern states and the beginning of the Civil War.

7. Many historians argue that the Civil War did not mark a change or break from America's past. They see the conflict as a continuation of the bitter sectional rivalries that characterized United States politics. The Missouri Compromise, the nullification crisis, and the violence in Kansas can all be used to support this argument.

8. Other historians argue that the Civil War represented an unprecedented breakdown of America's traditional, democratic political processes. The Deep South's refusal to accept the results of the 1860 presidential election can be used to support this argument.

THE CIVIL WAR

1. The Confederacy showed military initiative and daring early in the war. However, the Union ultimately prevailed because of its greater economic resources; strategic victories at Antietam, Gettysburg, and Vicksburg; and Lincoln's wartime leadership.

2. The secession of the Southern states enabled the Republicans to dominate Congress. They took advantage of their new position by enacting high tariffs, organizing a new banking system with a uniform currency, approving a transcontinental railroad, and passing a Homestead Act that opened the Great Plains to settlers.

3. Both Southern and Northern women accepted new responsibilities as more and more men left their homes and jobs to fight in the army. For example, planters' wives and daughters learned how to manage their plantations. In the North, women took paying jobs in business and government.

THE EMANCIPATION PROCLAMATION

1. The Union's narrow victory at Antietam enabled President Lincoln to turn his attention to the pressing issues of when and how to emancipate the South's four million slaves. By autumn 1862, Congress had already prohibited slavery in Washington, D.C. and the western territories. Lincoln feared that Britain and France would recognize the Confederacy unless the Union war aims included abolition as a moral cause.

2. President Lincoln issued the Emancipation Proclamation on January 1, 1863. The proclamation only applied to slaves in states or parts of states then in rebellion. It excluded freeing slaves in border states still within the Union and in other areas where Union forces were in control.

3. The Emancipation Proclamation widened the war into a crusade against slavery. With slavery now doomed, public opinion in Europe swung decisively behind the Union cause. The Emancipation Proclamation thus ended any chance that European powers would actively aid the Confederacy.

4. Lincoln considered the Emancipation Proclamation the crowning achievement of his presidency. "If my name ever goes into history," he declared, "it was for this act."

RECONSTRUCTION

1. The Thirteenth Amendment formally abolished slavery. But two centuries of slavery created deeply rooted racial prejudices that a Constitutional amendment could not eradicate.

2. Unwilling to accept blacks as equals, Southern states enacted laws known as Black Codes to link the freedmen's basic civil and legal rights. For example, Black Codes barred African Americans from carrying guns, marrying whites, assembling in groups, serving on juries, or pursuing any occupation other than agricultural work.

3. President Johnson did not object to the Black Codes. His lenient view of Reconstruction placed the president on a collision course with a Congress dominated by Radical Republicans who wanted to transform the South by extending civil and political rights to African Americans.

4. Radical Republicans promoted the Fourteenth Amendment to counter Johnson's lenient program and overturn the Black Codes. The first section granted citizenship to "all persons born or naturalized in the United States." This famous definition overturned the Dred Scott decision and the Three-Fifths Compromise.

5. The Fourteenth Amendment also prohibited the states from depriving "a person of life, liberty, or property, without due process of law; nor deny to any person within its jurisdiction equal protection of the laws."

6. After extensive debate, Congress ratified the Fifteenth Amendment. It forbade either the federal government or the states from denying citizens the right to vote on the basis of "race, color, or previous condition of servitude."

7. The Fifteenth Amendment enabled African American men to exercise political influence for the first time. Freedmen provided about 80 percent of the Republican votes in the South. Over 600 blacks served in reconstructed state legislatures. In addition, voters elected 14 blacks to the House of Representatives and two to the Senate.

8. The Fifteenth Amendment outraged feminist leaders. They demanded to know why Congress granted the suffrage to former slaves and not to women.

FROM SLAVE TO SHARECROPPER

1. Many former slaves stayed on their plantations because they could not afford to leave.

2. During the late 1860s, cotton planters and black freedmen entered into a new labor system called SHARECROPPING. Under this system, black families exchanged their labor for the use of the planter's land, tools, and seed. The sharecropper typically gave the landowner half of the crops as payment for the use of his property.

3. Sharecropping did not lead to economic independence. Unscrupulous landowners and shopkeepers charged sharecroppers exorbitant prices and unfair interest rates. This system of economic exploitation trapped African Americans in a seemingly endless cycle of debt and poverty.

THE RESTORATION OF WHITE SUPREMACY

1. White Southerners believed that vindictive Republicans sought to punish them by repealing Black Codes and enfranchising African Americans. The years following the end of the Civil War witnessed the proliferation of white supremacist organizations such as the Ku Klux Klan.

2. The Klan's reign of terror worked. As black voting declined, Democrats regained power. By 1876, Democrats replaced Republicans in eight of the eleven former Confederate states.

3. Republicans grew weary of pressing their agenda to reconstruct Southern society. Sympathy for the freedmen began to wane as radical leaders died or left office. A new generation of "politicos" began to focus their attention on Western expansion, wars with Native Americans, tariffs, and the construction of the transcontinental railroads.

4. The disputed 1876 presidential election provided an opportunity for the North to end Reconstruction. After tense negotiations, Democratic leaders agreed to support the Republican candidate, Rutherford Hays. In return, Hays agreed to adopt a "Let 'Em Alone Policy" that included the withdrawal of all federal troops from the South. The remaining Republican governments quickly collapsed as Southern Democrats proclaimed a return to "home rule" and white supremacy.

LOOKING IN-DEPTH
POLK AND MANIFEST DESTINY

As Andrew Jackson left the White House he confidently predicted that Americans were chosen by Providence to be "the guardians of freedom to preserve it for the benefit of the human race." The American people wholeheartedly agreed with Jackson. Convinced of the superiority of their customs and institutions, they believed that all their causes were just and that all their endeavors were moral. In short, what was good for America was good for everyone else.

As the United States reached across the wilderness toward the Pacific Ocean, Americans thought about and talked about expansion as though it was a great crusade. A New York newspaperman, John L. O'Sullivan gave the nation's expansionist spirit a name when he coined the term Manifest Destiny. O'Sullivan declared that America's claim to the land lay in the right of "our manifest destiny to occupy and to possess the whole of the continent which Providence has given us."

James K. Polk shared the confidence and ambition of the American people. When he was elected president in 1844, Americans had reached the nation's western boundaries. But California still belonged to Mexico and America and Great Britain still shared the Oregon Territory. The American people wanted these Pacific lands for their own and they elected Polk because he accepted the "Manifest Destiny" justification for national expansion.

Polk devoted his formidable energies to achieving the goal of fulfilling America's Manifest Destiny. He negotiated a compromise agreement with Great Britain that divided Oregon at the 49th parallel. He then instigated a successful war with Mexico. Under the terms of the Treaty of Guadalupe Hidalgo, Mexico relinquished all claims to Texas, California, and New Mexico.

So why should you remember Polk and Manifest Destiny? Do not expect to see questions about the missionaries and traders who blazed new trails to the West or the generals who conquered Mexico. Instead, make sure you can define Manifest Destiny, list the key provisions of the Treaty of Guadalupe Hidalgo and describe how winning the vast new western territories ignited an increasingly bitter dispute about the extension of slavery.

THE KANSAS–NEBRASKA ACT, 1854

APUSH textbooks accurately describe the passage of the Kansas-Nebraska Act as a momentous event in American history. In order to understand why this is true I'd like to briefly take you back to December 1853, just a month before Senator Stephen A. Douglas introduced his fateful Kansas-Nebraska bill. At that time most Americans believed that the Compromise of 1850 had settled the issue of slavery in the new western territories. The Democrats controlled the White House and Congress and were committed to maintaining the status quo. In December 1853 the Republican Party did not exist and the Missouri Compromise line separating free and slave states was viewed as a permanent agreement. But all this was about to dramatically and irrevocably change.

In January 1854, Senator Stephen A. Douglas of Illinois proposed a bill that would allow the settlers of Kansas and Nebraska to use popular sovereignty to decide whether or not slavery would be permitted within their borders. If enacted into law, Douglas' bill would repeal the Missouri Compromise by allowing slavery north of the 36° 30' line. Congress finally passed the Kansas-Nebraska Act after a bitter and divisive debate that lasted three and a half months.

The passage of the Kansas-Nebraska Act had immediate and profound consequences. The act reopened sectional issues and aroused public opinion in the North. It dealt the Whig Party a fatal blow. The national uproar over the Kansas-Nebraska Act galvanized anti-slavery into forming the new Republican Party, dedicated to keeping slavery out of the territories. And finally, the act energized Abraham Lincoln and transformed the then obscure former Whig Congressman from Illinois into a Republican Party leader.

So why should you remember the Kansas-Nebraska Act? Needless to say, many APUSH exams include a question about the act and its momentous consequences. So be sure you know that the Kansas-Nebraska Act repealed the Missouri Compromise, weakened the Democratic Party, destroyed the Whig Party, sparked the rise of the Republican Party and revived the political career of Abraham Lincoln.

NATIVISM AND THE KNOW-NOTHING PARTY

The story of the Know-Nothing Party actually begins in Ireland with the potato. First domesticated in Peru, the potato spread to Ireland where it became a staple crop among the poor. By 1845 one-third of the Irish population depended upon their potato crop for survival. In that year a blight ravaged the Irish potato crop. The blight caused a severe famine that killed at least 1 million people. Over 1.5 million desperate and impoverished Irish fled to America.

Most Irish immigrants settled in the fast-growing port cities along the Northeast coast. The Irish immigrants were overwhelmingly Roman Catholics whose religious ceremonies and black robed priests and nuns seemed strange and threatening to native-born Protestants. Many Americans stereotyped the Irish as ignorant and clannish people who would never assimilate into American life.

The great wave of Irish immigration sparked a nativist, or anti-foreign, reaction. Fearing that the Irish would have a deleterious influence upon American culture, nativists formed societies with the political goal of restricting immigration and making naturalization a much longer process. Nativist groups like the Order of United Americans and the Order of the Star-Spangled Banner were organized like lodges, complete with special handshakes and passwords. When members were questioned about the purpose of their secret group they usually replied, "I know nothing." The suspicious nativists were popularly known as the Know-Nothings.

The Know-Nothings soon formed a political party that directed its hostility toward Catholic immigrants from Ireland and Germany. The party platform demanded laws that would allow only native-born Americans to hold political office. Know-Nothing candidates enjoyed initial success. The party captured over 40 congressional seats in the 1854 election. Its 1856 presidential candidate Millard Filmore won 21 percent of the popular vote and 8 electoral votes. However, the Know-Nothings electoral success proved to be fleeting. The anti-Catholic fervor subsided as immigration declined and the country shifted its focus to the great national debate over slavery.

So why should you remember the Know-Nothing Party? The Know-Nothings were America's first nativist political party. Although the party soon disappeared, it marked the beginning of a recurring pattern of nativist opposition to immigrants.

THE BLACK CODES, 1866

The months immediately following the Civil War were a period of great uncertainty. The defeated Southern states promptly ratified the Thirteenth Amendment ending slavery. However, they still faced difficult questions about the future place of over 4 million newly-freed slaves in Southern society.

Slavery left a legacy of prejudice and discrimination that would be difficult to eliminate. Unwilling to accept black Americans as equals, each Southern legislature enacted laws known as Black Codes to limit the freedmen's basic civil and economic rights. This continued the legal distinction between black and white Americans. For example, laws barred black people from carrying weapons, marrying whites, assembling in groups, serving on juries, and pursuing any occupation other than agricultural work.

President Johnson did not object to the Black Codes. His lenient view of Reconstruction placed the President on a collision course with a Congress dominated by Radical Republicans. Led by Thaddeus Stevens and Charles Sumner, Congress insisted that the basic rights of African Americans be protected. Congress promptly passed the Civil Rights Act of 1866 which declared that all persons born in the United States were American citizens who enjoyed equality before the law.

Johnson stunned Congress by vetoing the Civil Rights Act. His veto infuriated the Republicans who quickly overrode the president's veto. The struggle over the Black Codes and the Civil Rights Act led to a number of far-reaching consequences. It marked the beginning of a contest of wills between Johnson and Congress that ended with an impeachment trial. It also prompted Congress to pass the Fourteenth Amendment. This landmark amendment overturned the Dred Scott decision by making the former slaves citizens. It also invalidated the Black Codes by forbidding a state from denying "any person within its jurisdiction the equal protection of the laws."

So why should you remember the Black Codes? APUSH test writers will expect you to know that the Black Codes limited the basic human rights and civil liberties of the newly freed black people. They will also expect you to know that the Black Codes played an important role in bringing about the impeachment of President Johnson and the passage of the Fourteenth Amendment.

CHAPTER 6
PERIOD 6
1876 – 1898

TIMELINE

1869   Completion of the first transcontinental railroad

1876   Alexander Graham Bell invents the telephone

1882   Chinese Exclusion Act

1882   John D. Rockefeller forms the Standard Oil Trust

1886   Formation of American Federation of Labor (AFL)

1887   Dawes Act

1889   Jane Addams founds Hull House in Chicago

1890   Battle of Wounded Knee

1890   Wave of New Immigrants pours into America

1890   Jacob Riis publishes *How the Other Half Lives*

1893   Chicago World Columbian Exposition opens

1895   Booker T. Washington delivers Atlanta Compromise speech

1896   "Separate but equal" decision in *Plessy v. Ferguson* promotes segregation

1896   Demise of the Populist Party as Republican win the presidential election

WESTWARD EXPANSION

1. The completion of the first transcontinental railroad marked the beginning of an economic boom across the West. The network of transcontinental lines created a vast integrated national market for raw materials and manufactured goods.

2. The Homestead Act of 1862 and the completion of the transcontinental railroad opened the West to agriculture. In the 30 years between 1870 and

1900, more land was made into farms than in all the previous 250 years. The population of the Great Plains steadily increased as 600,000 people settled in Kansas. By 1890, over 500,000 African Americans lived west of the Mississippi River.

3. The construction of the transcontinental railroad, the slaughter of the buffalo, the spread of epidemic diseases, and the destructive effect of constant warfare all threatened the autonomy of the Plains Indians.

4. Treaties between the United States government and Native Americans usually lasted a short time before being broken by settlers' incursions onto Native American reservations.

5. The Dawes Act tried to "civilize" the Plains tribes by turning them into independent, self-supporting farmers. The act ignored the importance traditional indigenous cultures placed upon tribally held land. Instead of transforming Native Americans into self-supporting farmers, the Dawes Act undermined their culture and cost them their land.

6. The Ghost Dance aroused erroneous fears that Native Americans intended to go on a warpath. The army's overreaction led to the tragic loss of life at the Battle of Wounded Knee.

7. The Bureau of Indian Affairs subjected Plains Indian children to a policy of FORCED ASSIMILATION intended to "Americanize" Native American children. Reform groups opened boarding schools that isolated indigenous children from their tribes. Teachers tried to "Americanize" students by focusing on American cultural practices while simultaneously compelling them to give up their indigenous culture, spiritual beliefs, and even their names.

8. American historians have traditionally viewed western expansion as a positive force that shaped American ideas and policies during the second half of the nineteenth century. For example, in his influential essay, "The Significance of the Frontier in American History," Frederick Jackson Turner forcefully portrays western expansion as essential to the development of American character and the frontier spirit. He pointed out that the United States brought railroads, towns, the telegraph, the herding of cattle, and widespread agriculture to the West.

9. In contrast, contemporary historians, such as Patricia Nelson Limerick, view western expansion as characterized by conquest, intermixing, and division. In her book *The Legacy of Conquest*, Limerick forcefully portrays western expansion as a series of challenges and uneasy bargains among a diverse group of Native Americans, White Americans, African Americans, and Latinos. According to Limerick, the forcible conquest and annexation of the

West were expressions of American expansionism and imperialism, which had consequences antithetical to the democratic spirit.

THE "NEW SOUTH"

1. Henry Grady, editor of the *Atlanta Constitution*, called for a "New South" that would be home to thriving cities, bustling factories, and rewarding business opportunities. A new generation of Southern entrepreneurs sought to fulfill Grady's vision by building a more diversified regional economy. New textile mills in the Carolinas and steel mills in Birmingham, Alabama, helped spur industrial growth. However, the dream of a New South remained elusive. Despite pockets of industrial development, Grady's goal of a diversified Southern economy remained elusive.

2. In 1900, two-thirds of all Southern men still earned their living as farmers. During the 1860s, cotton planters and black farmers formed a new labor arrangement called SHARECROPPING. The system's exchange of black labor for the use of white-owned land did not lead to economic independence. Instead, black Americans became entrapped in a seemingly endless cycle of debt and poverty.

3. Efforts to change Southern racial attitudes and culture ultimately failed because of the South's determined resistance and the North's waning resolve.

4. The end of Reconstruction left political control in the South in the hands of Democratic Party leaders collectively known as Redeemers because they claimed to redeem or save the South from Republican rule. The Redeemers were committed to white supremacy.

5. Redeemer governments used literacy tests and poll taxes to evade the Fifteenth Amendment. These tactics worked. During the 1890s, the number of black voters plummeted.

6. The Supreme Court decision in *Plessy v. Ferguson* upheld "separate but equal" railroad facilities for African Americans. *Plessy v. Ferguson* allowed Jim Crow segregation laws to spread across the South.

7. Booker T. Washington opposed public agitation to fight Jim Crow laws. Instead, he urged African Americans to follow a policy of accommodation by accepting segregation, avoiding public controversies, and concentrating on economic advancement. In his "Atlanta Compromise Speech," Washington offered a conciliatory approach welcomed by his white audience: "In all things purely social we can be as separate as the fingers, yet one as the hand in all things essential to mutual progress."

THE RISE OF INDUSTRIAL CAPITALISM

1. America's railroad network increased from 35,000 miles in 1865 to 193,000 miles in 1900. Railroad construction stimulated industrial growth by consuming vast quantities of iron, steel, coal, and lumber. The enormous expansion of rail lines facilitated an unprecedented movement of people, products, and ideas.

2. Prior to the Civil War, wood provided about half of America's energy needs. However, during the postwar period coal played a key role in the rise of industrial capitalism. American railroads and steamships took the lead in replacing wood with coal. In addition, steel mills used vast quantities of coal to fire their furnaces.

3. Railroads, steel companies, and oil refineries all faced intense competition from ambitious rivals. During the 1880s and 1890s, corporate executives consolidated their businesses into huge trusts and holding companies. By 1900, enormous corporations dominated the steel, oil, sugar, and meat-packing industries.

4. Industrial capitalism produced a number of significant benefits. Efficient mass production methods reduced prices and gave consumers access to cheaper commodities. Booming corporations hired thousands of foremen, managers, and engineers who became part of a rising middle class.

5. America's booming economy concentrated unprecedented wealth in the hands of a small but powerful group of industrial titans. By 1900, the richest two percent of American households owned over one-third of the nation's wealth.

6. SOCIAL DARWINISM was a set of beliefs that both explained and justified how a small group of business and industrial leaders could accumulate great wealth. Social Darwinists believed that Darwin's law of natural selection could be applied to individuals, corporations, and nations. According to Social Darwinists, individuals and corporations are engaged in a ruthless struggle for profit in which only the fittest survive and prosper.

7. Andrew Carnegie was an ardent supporter of Social Darwinism. However, Carnegie also believed that great wealth brought great responsibility. In his influential essay, "The Gospel of Wealth," Carnegie encouraged philanthropists to support public libraries, universities, museums, and other "ladders upon which the aspiring can rise."

LABOR UNIONS IN THE GILDED AGE

1. Owners enjoyed enormous profits while their workers earned meager salaries. America's poorly paid workers were also unprotected by safety regulations.

2. Founded in 1869, the Knights of Labor attempted to unify all working men and women into a national union under the motto, "An injury to one is the concern of all." After a period of rapid growth, the Knights began to lose influence when newspapers unjustly blamed them for causing the Haymarket Square riot. The union's membership declined as the public erroneously linked the Knights with violent anarchists who opposed all forms of government.

3. Founded in 1886, the American Federation of Labor (AFL) was an alliance of skilled workers and craft unions. Unlike the Knights of Labor, the AFL did not welcome unskilled workers, women, or racial minorities. Led by Samuel Gompers, the AFL focused on bread-and-butter issues such as wages and working conditions.

4. The AFL's commitment to craft unions excluded many workers. Like the Knights of Labor, the Industrial Workers of the World (or Wobblies) attempted to unite all skilled and unskilled workers. While the AFL focused on bread-and-butter issues, the Industrial Workers of the World focused on what one of its leaders called "the irresistible conflict between the capitalist class and the working class."

5. The Great Railroad Strike of 1877 signaled the beginning of a period of strikes and violent confrontations between labor and management. Between 1880 and 1900 over 23,000 strikes, the most in the industrial world, disrupted the American economy.

6. President Cleveland called out federal troops to break the Pullman strike on the grounds that it obstructed the ability of trains to deliver the U.S. mail. The Pullman Strike demonstrated that the federal government would actively intervene to crush strikes and protect management.

THE NEW IMMIGRANTS

1. Prior to the 1890s, most new Americans came from Western European countries such as England, Ireland, and Germany. But beginning in the 1890s, ethnic groups known as NEW IMMIGRANTS began to arrive from countries in Southern and Eastern Europe such as Italy, Poland, and Russia. The overwhelming majority practiced the Roman Catholic and Jewish faiths.

2. The new immigrants fled religious persecution, oppressive governments, and hopeless poverty. Pushed by intolerance and hardship, the new immigrants were pulled by America's booming industrial economy. The new immigrants were attracted to America by more than just jobs; they also coveted America as a land offering a new life. The view of the Statue of Liberty lifting her torch of freedom filled the new arrivals with a sense of hope.

3. The harsh realities of life and work in America soon tempered the new immigrant's initial optimism. The overwhelming majority of newcomers gravitated to ethnic enclaves in Northeastern and Midwestern cities. Lacking financial resources, one-third stayed in New York City. The city's Lower East Side contained 334,000 people, making it one of the most densely populated places in the world.

4. Jacob Riis used his pioneering photographic skill to document the hardship of life in Lower East Side tenements, streets, and alleys. His poignant photographs of impoverished children opened affluent New Yorkers' eyes to a world they had previously ignored.

5. In 1890, Riis compiled his photographs and graphic commentary into an influential book, *How the Other Half Lives*. The powerful work galvanized a new generation of Progressive reformers.

THE REVIVAL OF NATIVIST SENTIMENT

1. The wave of Irish and German immigrants in the 1840s sparked a NATIVIST, or anti-foreign, reaction among native-born Protestants.

2. The wave of new immigrants from Southern and Eastern Europe provoked an even stronger nativist response.

3. Nativists warned that the new immigrants would not assimilate or become like Americans of an earlier time.

4. The Immigrant Restriction League (IRL) took advantage of America's growing climate of anxiety and suspicion. Formed in Boston in 1894, the IRL advanced the pseudo-scientific theory that each ethnic group had its own inborn characteristics. For example, Anglo-Saxons possess courage and leadership skills, placing them at the top of the ethnic pyramid. In contrast, Italians were a violent and undisciplined ethnic group incapable of assimilating American culture.

5. Although nativist groups were initially unsuccessful in their attempts to limit immigration from Southern and Eastern Europe, they were able to block Chinese immigration into California and the West Coast.

6. First attracted by the Gold Rush, Chinese immigrants quickly became the largest non-European group living in California. Working-class white Californians bitterly complained that Chinese laborers provided unfair competition because they worked for low wages.

7. Congress responded to the nativist outcry by passing the Chinese Exclusion Act in 1882. The act prohibited Chinese workers from entering the United States.

8. The Chinese Exclusion Act marked America's first law designed to exclude a specific ethnic or racial group from immigrating to the United States.

THE SOCIAL GOSPEL MOVEMENT

1. The SOCIAL GOSPEL movement focused on building a just society by addressing pressing urban and industrial problems. Advocates of the Social Gospel believed that American churches had a moral responsibility to take the lead in actively confronting social problems and helping the urban poor.

2. Walter Rauschenbusch was a theologian and Baptist minister who emerged as one of the key figures in the Social Gospel movement. His sermons and books urged his followers to use direct social action to rectify the social sins plaguing American society.

3. Rauschenbusch strongly opposed Social Darwinism's belief that the fittest will survive and prosper while the unfit and lazy deserve their fate and should not receive help from society. In contrast, Rauschenbusch insisted that society has a moral responsibility to help the poor and less fortunate.

4. The Social Gospel movement added energy and a sense of urgency to the emerging Progressive movement. Inspired by the Social Gospel message, Jane Addams transformed a decaying mansion located in the heart of one of Chicago's poorest immigrant neighborhoods into a thriving settlement house, offering services such as day care, English lessons, and personal hygiene. Hull House became a model that inspired the founding of over 400 similar facilities across America.

5. Many historians argue that the Social Gospel movement constitutes a distinctive Third Great Awakening. They point out that the First Great Awakening focused largely on redeeming the souls of individual sinners. The Second Great Awakening focused on both individual salvation and social sins such as alcoholism and slavery. In contrast, the Third Great Awakening galvanized American Protestants to address the plight of impoverished people living in urban slums.

BIG CITY POLITICAL MACHINES

1. Tightly organized groups of politicians, popularly called machines, controlled many big-city governments.

2. The machines had a strong centralized organization. Power flowed from a boss down through several levels of command, ending in a ward or neighborhood.

3. Ward politicians worked hard to win votes. For example, they provided needed social services by helping immigrant families find places to live and by providing them with baskets of food.

4. Above all, political bosses rewarded loyal followers with government jobs called patronage. They proudly boasted, "To the victors belong the spoils!"

5. New York City fell under the control of a particularly corrupt machine led by Boss Tweed. The venal boss confidently boasted, "As long as I count the votes, what are you going to do about it?" Tweed and his cronies stole as much as $200 million from the public treasury.

6. Tweed's reign of unbridled greed and theft finally came to an end from an unlikely source. Thomas Nast exposed Tweed's fraudulent practices in a series of political cartoons that mercilessly portrayed the Tweed Ring as a group of thieves and scoundrels.

THE POPULIST REVOLT

1. American farmers increasingly saw themselves as victims of an unjust economic and political system. They believed government *laissez-faire* policies allowed unregulated corporations to exercise too much power over their lives and livelihoods.

2. Western farmers directed special anger at the railroads. They accused the railroads of abusing their monopoly by charging exorbitant freight rates. At the same time, they assailed government economic policies that limited the money supply by mandating that the nation's currency had to be backed by gold.

3. Silverites believed the free coinage of silver would increase the money supply, raise commodity prices, and alleviate farm debts.

4. As their debts mounted, struggling farmers became convinced that neither the Democratic nor the Republican parties would address the problems caused by greedy bankers and arrogant railroad executives.

5. In 1892 the wave of agrarian discontent gave birth to the People's, or Populist Party. The Populists hoped to build a coalition of Western and

Southern farmers and Eastern industrial workers that would replace the Democrats as a major political party.

6. The Populist Party platform called for a stronger federal government role in the nation's economy. Specific demands included government control of the railroads, free coinage of silver, a graduated income tax, and the direct election of United States senators.

7. Critics charged that the Populist platform comprised an unwieldly collection of impractical ideas. However, the Populists achieved surprising successes in the 1892 presidential election.

8. The 1896 presidential election featured a dramatic contest between William McKinley and William Jennings Bryan. McKinley and the Republicans supported the gold standard and high tariffs. Supported by both the Populists and the Democrats, Bryan voiced vigorous support for free silver.

9. McKinley's victory produced a number of important consequences. Bryan's defeat led to the swift collapse of the Populist Party. The election of 1896 began a generation of almost unbroken Republican dominance that lasted until the election of Franklin Roosevelt in 1932. However, the defeat of the Populists did not end the spirit of reform. A new generation of Progressive reformers endorsed constitutional amendments calling for a graduated income tax and the direct election of senators.

10.   Coxey's Army was a protest march by unemployed workers led by Ohio businessman Jacob Coxey. The desperate workers supported Coxey's proposal to put the nation's jobless to work building roads and other construction projects. Coxey and his followers marched to Washington, D.C. in 1894 during the depths of a sharp economic depression. Like other Populists, Coxey advocated government action to relieve depressed conditions. Although Coxey's proposal for government action was too radical for its time, it became part of US policy during the New Deal.

LOOKING IN-DEPTH
THE GREAT RAILROAD STRIKE OF 1877

Let me begin by asking you a question: Which 19th Century labor strike caused the most property damage, involved the most workers, claimed the most lives, and required the most soldiers to restore order? Many APUSH students would probably answer either the Homestead Strike or the Pullman Strike. However, the correct answer is the Great Railroad Strike of 1877. Although often overlooked by APUSH texts and teachers, the Great Railroad Strike is attracting increased attention from APUSH test writers.

The immediate cause of the Great Railroad Strike can be traced to the economic depression that followed the Panic of 1877. As business slumped, the railroads cut salaries and hours. In 1877 both the Pennsylvania Railroad and the Baltimore and Ohio Railroad slashed wages by 10 percent. Driven by anger and despair, desperate railroad workers near Baltimore walked off their jobs and refused to allow trains to run in any direction.

The strike quickly followed the rail lines to Pittsburgh, Kansas City, St. Louis, Chicago and San Francisco. As the strike rippled across the country it paralyzed the nation's commerce for 45 days. Looters and rioters destroyed millions of dollars of property. Alarmed by the spreading violence, governors called out 60,000 state militia and President Hays ordered federal troops to crush the strike and restore law and order.

The Great Railroad Strike of 1877 left a bitter legacy of death and destruction. Over 100,000 striking workers disrupted rail commerce across the entire nation. Clashes with soldiers claimed over 100 lives and left hundreds injured.

So why should you remember the Great Railroad Strike of 1877? The strike marked an explosion of firsts. It was America's first major railroad strike and the country's first national strike. It was also the first major strike broken by the US military. The Great Railroad Strike of 1877 signaled the beginning of a period of strikes and violent confrontations between labor and management that continued throughout the 1880s and 1890s.

THE DAWES ACT, 1887

The Dawes Act became law on February 8, 1887. Reformers promptly hailed the legislation as the "Indian Emancipation Act." The Secretary of the Interior joined the chorus of well-meaning supporters by calling the Dawes Act, "the most important measure ever enacted in this country affecting Indian affairs."

The reformers who worked so hard to persuade Congress to enact the Dawes Act would be very surprised to know that modern critics view the law as a disastrous example of forced assimilation. So why was the Dawes Act passed and why was it a failure?

The construction of the transcontinental railroads, the slaughter of the buffalo, and the government's reservation policy all dealt devastating blows to the culture of the Plains Indians. These policies outraged Helen Hunt Jackson and prompted her to investigate the government's record of dealing with Native Americans. Her book, *A Century of Dishonor*, chronicled the government's disgraceful record of ruthlessness and chicanery in treating Native Americans.

The accusations in *A Century of Dishonor* helped mobilize public support for a new Indian policy. Well-meaning but ethnocentric reformers believed that the Native Americans' traditional tribal culture was an obstacle preventing them from assimilating into mainstream white society. The Dawes Act attempted to "civilize" Native Americans by turning them into independent, self-supporting farmers. The act dissolved the tribes as legal entities and divided their lands into individual homesteads of 160 acres. These homesteads would then be distributed to the head of each family. "Excess" reservation lands not allocated to Native American families were then sold as "surplus" to the railroads and to white settlers.

The Dawes Act ignored the importance traditional indigenous culture placed on tribally held land. Instead of transforming Native Americans into self-supporting farmers, the act undermined their traditional culture and cost them their land. By 1900 Native Americans lost 50 percent of the 156 million acres they held before the Dawes Act became law.

So why should you remember the Dawes Act? The legislation illustrated how the government's policy of forced assimilation undermined traditional tribal cultures. Forced assimilation became the cornerstone of the government's official Indian policy until it was finally reversed by the Indian Reorganization Act of 1934.

PLESSY V. FERGUSON, 1896

During the late 1880s, Southern states had not yet erected the legal walls of Jim Crow segregation. At that time, racial discrimination was erratic and inconsistent. For example, the usual practice on trains was to exclude black people from first class cars but allow them to mingle with whites on "smoking" cars.

The age of Jim Crow segregation began to arrive in Louisiana with the passage of the Separate Car Act in 1890. The law required railroads "to provide equal but separate accommodations for the white and colored races." Outraged by the law, black people in New Orleans formed a Citizens Committee to test the legality of the Separate Car Act.

On June 7, 1892, Homer Plessy bought a train ticket from New Orleans to Covington, Louisiana. Plessy was born a free man and was known to have had a black great-grandmother. Although he was seven-eighths Caucasian, the Separate Car Act classified Plessy as black and required him to sit in a "colored car." Plessy deliberately defied the law by sitting in a white-only car. A detective immediately arrested Plessy when he refused to move to the "colored car."

Supported by the New Orleans Citizens Committee, Plessy filed a suit against the railroad. He argued that the Separate Car Act violated the equal protection clause of the Fourteenth Amendment. However, Judge John H. Ferguson of New Orleans ruled against Plessy. When the Louisiana Supreme Court upheld Ferguson's decision, the Citizen's Committee appealed the case to the United States Supreme Court.

Plessy's legal team argued that the Separate Car Act placed an unnecessary and unjust "badge of inferiority" on African Americans. They asked the Supreme Court justices to consider how they would react if the legal tables were turned and they had to sit in Jim Crow cars. They forcefully emphasized that, "Justice is pictured blind and her daughter, the Law, ought at least to be color-blind." Unmoved by these arguments, the Supreme Court ruled against Plessy by a 7 to 1 vote. The Court's decision upheld racial segregation by approving "separate but equal" railroad facilities for African Americans.

So why should you remember *Plessy v. Ferguson*? The ruling allowed Jim Crow segregation laws to spread across the South. Soon there were segregated schools, restaurants, and hotels. Ubiquitous signs declaring "White Only" or "Colored" appeared on restroom doors, above water fountains, and inside stores. *Plessy v. Ferguson* remained the law of the land until it was finally reversed by the landmark Supreme Court decision in *Brown v. Board of Education*.

THE PRESIDENTIAL ELECTION OF 1896

Do presidential elections matter? Cynics often claim that America's presidential elections typically offer a choice between Twiddle Dee and Twiddle Dum. But this criticism was definitely not valid for the election of 1896 when both the Republicans and the Democrats believed that the future of America was very much at stake.

The Republicans met in St. Louis and nominated William McKinley, the affable and well-liked governor of Ohio. McKinley supported both the gold standard and high protective tariffs. The gold standard linked money to this scarce precious metal so that debtors never got a break from inflation. Tariffs protected capitalists and their workers from foreign competition.

The Democrats met in Chicago and nominated William Jennings Bryan, a 36-year-old former Congressman from Nebraska. Bryan was committed to a policy of free silver that would devalue money and help debtors. In a famous speech, Bryan galvanized cheering delegates by defiantly warning wealthy creditors, "You shall not crucify mankind upon a crown of Gold."

The charismatic Bryan broke with tradition by crisscrossing the country and taking his campaign directly to the people. He delivered over 600 speeches in 26 states, extolling the benefits of free silver. Meanwhile, McKinley stayed in Canton, Ohio, and ran a "front porch" campaign adroitly managed by his close friend Mark Hanna. Friendly rail road companies provided reduced fares enabling 750,000 people to visit Canton and hear McKinley promise "good work, good wages, and good money."

Bryan won the battle of speeches but McKinley won the fight for votes. The Republicans won an overwhelming victory in the Northeast and Midwest. McKinley triumphed by a margin of 271 to 176 in the Electoral College. Nearly 80 percent of the eligible electorate voted in one of the highest turnouts ever.

So why should you remember the Election of 1896? The election of 1896 led to the swift collapse of the pro-silver Populist Party. At the same time, it began a generation of almost unbroken Republican dominance that lasted until the election of Franklin D. Roosevelt in 1932.

JACOB RIIS AND JANE ADDAMS

I'd like to begin by asking you an easy question: Who has generated the most APUSH questions: George Washington and Dwight Eisenhower or Jacob Riis and Jane Addams? The answer is Jacob Riis and Jane Addams. It is always important to remember that social reformers take precedence over victorious generals on the APUSH exam.

Jacob Riis was an early muckraking journalist and social documentary photographer. His book, *How the Other Half Lives*, exposed the harsh living conditions endured by New Immigrants living in Manhattan's Lower East Side. Riis' poignant pictures and vivid eyewitness descriptions publicized the squalid housing conditions in New York City's densely crowded tenements. *How the Other Half Lives* prompted a public outcry that led to a decade of improvements in sewers, garbage collection, and indoor plumbing.

Jane Addams also chose to focus on improving the condition of the urban poor. Like many other women reformers, Addams grew up in an affluent home. She graduated from college in 1881 filled with ambition but still lacking a cause. Addams found her calling eight years later when she rented a run-down mansion in Chicago that had belonged to a man named Charles Hull. Addams transformed Hull House into America's first urban settlement house. The facility rapidly expanded and ultimately included day care nurseries, English lessons, and a number of practical courses on cooking, dressmaking, and hygiene. Hull House served as a model for other middle-class women who founded over 400 settlement houses in cities across America.

So why should you remember Jacob Riis and Jane Addams? The obvious answer is because both have generated a significant number of multiple-choice questions on APUSH exams. In addition, you should remember Jacob Riis and Jane Addams because both were pioneering social reformers who successfully addressed problems faced by the New Immigrants.

CHAPTER 7
PERIOD 7
1890 – 1945

TIMELINE

1898   War between the United States and Spain

1898   The United States annexes Hawaii, the Philippines, Puerto Rico, and Guam

1901   McKinley assassinated; Theodore Roosevelt assumes presidency

1915   German submarine sinks the *Lusitania*

1917   United States enters World War I

1920   The Nineteenth Amendment grants women suffrage

1920   Height of the Red Scare

1920   Beginning of the Harlem Renaissance

1924   National Origins Act

1929   Stock Market crashes precipitating the Great Depression

1933   FDR launches the First New Deal

1941   Japan attacks Pearl Harbor

1942   FDR signs an Executive Order moving Japanese to internment camps

1944   D-Day landing in France

1945   Germany and Japan surrender

1945   U.S. drops atomic bomb on Hiroshima and Nagasaki

THE ROOTS OF IMPERIALISM

1. In 1890, the United States still played a minor role in the global game of power politics. Then, in less than a decade, America became an imperial republic with interests in the Caribbean, Latin America, and the Pacific.

2. Business leaders worried that their factories were producing more goods than Americans could buy. Many corporate executives looked to Latin America, Asia, and the Pacific for new markets and new sources of raw materials.

3. IMPERIALISM is the policy of extending a nation's power through military conquest, economic domination, and/or territorial annexation. Advocates of imperialism argued that America's compelling economic need for raw materials and markets required it to play a more aggressive role in world affairs.

4. Captain Alfred T. Mahan published *The Influence of Sea Power upon History* in 1890. Mahan's book played an influential role in shaping late nineteenth- century American policy toward the importance of sea power.

5. Theodore Roosevelt, Senator Henry Cabot Lodge, and Alfred Mahan were all influential expansionists who argued that the United States must build a strong Navy, construct a canal through Central America, acquire fueling stations in the Pacific, and gain possessions in the Caribbean.

6. Other expansionists argued that America had a moral duty to bring the blessings of its civilization to less advanced peoples. Often called "The White Mans's Burden," this idea justified a new national mission to "elevate backward peoples."

CONSEQUENCES OF THE SPANISH–AMERICAN WAR

1. America quickly defeated Spain in a "splendid little war" that lasted just 114 days. The Spanish-American War marked the emergence of the United States as a world power.

2. The Treaty of Paris (1898) ceded Puerto Rico and Guam to the United States. Spain recognized Cuban independence and agreed to cede the Philippines to the United States for $20 million.

3. The provision of the Treaty of Paris ceding the Philippines to the United States aroused a strong anti-imperialist movement to block ratification of the treaty. The Anti-Imperialist League argued that controlling the Philippines would be contrary to America's long-standing commitment to human freedom and rule by the "consent of the people."

4. After a heated debate, the Senate approved the Treaty of Paris by just one vote.

5. The acquisition of the Philippines led to a bloody guerilla war. Led by Emilo Aguinaldo, the rebels protested the contradiction between America's revolutionary ideals and its policy of depriving self-government to the Philippine people.

THE PROGRESSIVES

1. After the collapse of the Populist Party, the reform spirit shifted to the cities, where a new generation of well educated, middle- and upper-middle-class reformers focused on a broad range of problems caused by industrialization and urbanization. Unlike the Populists, the Progressives did not initially form a third party. Instead, Progressivism embraced a widespread, multi-faceted movement to build a more democratic and just society. The Progressive Era is usually dated from 1890 to America's entry into World War I in 1917.

2. The Progressives rejected *laissez-faire,* or "hands off," government policies. Instead, they wanted government to play an active role in public life. The Progressives believed that complex social problems required a broad range of governmental responses. "The real heart of the movement," declared one Progressive, "was to use the government as an agency of human welfare."

3. The Progressives were idealists who rejected Social Darwinism. They believed conflict and ruthlessness would not improve society. Instead, they optimistically believed informed citizens could create a just society that would confront the plight of the urban poor, regulate corporations, protect the environment, address consumer issues, ,and elect honest leaders.

4. MUCKRAKERS were journalists who exposed corruption and social problems through investigative reporting. For example, Upton Sinclair's *The Jungle* used nauseating details to describe unsanitary practices in the meatpacking industry. His description of rats running across piles of warehouse meat provoked a national outcry. Congress responded to public pressure by enacting the Pure Food and Drug Act and the Meat Inspection Act to restore proper sanitation standards. These two acts illustrate the relationship between muckraking and reform legislation.

5. The Progressive Era marked a significant turning point in the history of American women. When the era began, men ran the nation's businesses and cast all of its votes. The prevailing belief in the cult of domesticity restricted women to their homes. During the Progressive Era a generation of middle-class "New Women" extended their role as guardians of the home to include becoming activists who fought to improve their local communities. Women became a driving force behind many Progressive Era reforms. They joined clubs, founded settlement houses, and successfully

fought for constitutional amendments prohibiting the sale of alcoholic beverages and granting women the suffrage.

6. Theodore Roosevelt quickly became a major voice in the Progressive movement. Like other Progressives, TR believed that government should be used to solve the nation's pressing problems. The dynamic force of his personality revitalized the presidency and established the White House as the focal point of American life. During his administration, TR launched antitrust action against the Northern Securities Company and secured passage of the Hepburn Act to regulate the railroads.

7. The wanton exploitation of western forests, wildlife, and scenic areas outraged Progressives. PRESERVATIONISTS believed that government policies should preserve wilderness areas in their natural state. In contrast, CONSERVATIONISTS believed that government policies should promote the management of natural resources in a responsible and sustained manner. TR embraced both views. As a Preservationist, he set aside more Federal land for natural parks and wildlife preserves than all of his predecessors combined. As a Conservationist, he signed the Newlands Reclamation Act that funded irrigation projects throughout the West.

8. Woodrow Wilson successfully implemented his Progressive New Freedom program by reducing tariffs, creating the Federal Reserve System, and strengthening antitrust laws.

9. Progressive Era reforms devoted little attention to the plight of African Americans. However, the era did witness the formation of the National Association for the Advancement of Colored People (NAACP) and the emergence of W.E.B. Du Bois as an influential black leader.

10.   Du Bois represented a younger generation of African Americans who criticized Booker T. Washington's commitment to gradual progress. In his groundbreaking book *The Souls of Black Folk*, Du Bois charged that Washington's strategy of accommodation would only serve to perpetuate segregation and racial injustice. He advanced an alternative program of "ceaseless agitation" to challenge Jim Crow segregation and demand full economic, social, and political equality.

THE ROAD TO WAR

1. President Wilson wanted to keep America out of the First World War. However, at the same time, he insisted on protecting American neutral rights on the high seas.

2. On May 7, 1915, a German submarine sank the *Lusitania*, a British passenger liner. About 1,200 people died, including 128 Americans. The sinking of the Lusitania forcibly raised the issue of freedom of the seas while also raising the issue of American military preparedness.

3. The United States entered the First World War on April 2, 1917, as a direct result of Germany's resumption of unrestricted submarine warfare.

4. The United States fought with Great Britain and France against a coalition of Central Powers that included Germany, Austria-Hungary, the Ottoman Empire, and Bulgaria.

5. The American Expeditionary Forces helped tip the balance of the conflict in favor of the Allies.

WWI: KEY HOMEFRONT DEVELOPMENTS

1. In 1900, nine out of every ten black Americans lived in the South, and three out of four worked on farms. The humiliation of Jim Crow segregation crushed the brief spirit of optimism following Emancipation. Grinding poverty along with the Ku Klux Klan's relentless campaign of intimidation and violence provided compelling reasons for African Americans in the South to leave their homes.

2. The outbreak of the First World War created a tremendous demand for wartime supplies. At that same time, the war curbed the flow of European immigrants to America. Northern assembly lines, steel mills, and meatpacking companies recruited African Americans from the South to fill the shortage of jobs.

3. The push of discrimination and the pull of a booming Northern job market convinced about 1.5 million African Americans to leave the South in the years between 1910 and 1930. This mass migration from the rural South to urban areas in the North and Midwest is known as the GREAT MIGRATION.

4. The First World War focused public attention on the war effort. Led by George Creel, the Committee of Public Information mobilized public opinion to support the troops by buying war bonds and suppressing dissent.

5. Wilson's Fourteen Points expressed the hopes of people for a just settlement that would ensure a lasting peace. His fourteenth and most famous point called for a League of Nations that would mediate disputes, supervise arms reductions, and curb aggressive nations through collective military action.

6. Wilson faced a difficult fight to win Senate approval for the Treaty of Versailles' provision for a League of Nations. Senate opponents objected to the League's collective security clause, arguing it would limit American

sovereignty, undermine the power of Congress in foreign affairs, and violate Washington's Farewell Address admonishment to avoid entangling foreign alliances.

7. In November 1917, Bolsheviks led by Vladimir Lenin seized power in Russia and promptly created a communist dictatorship. The revolutionary upheaval in Russia alarmed many Americans who believed communist sympathizers and other radicals were secretly planning to undermine the United States government.

8. A RED SCARE, or nationwide fear of aliens, swept across the country. Nearly 30 states enacted sedition laws, imposing harsh penalties on those who promoted revolution. Authorities sentenced 300 people to jail. Their only crime had been opposing the war.

9. Although no more than one-tenth of one percent of adult Americans belonged to the domestic communist movement, Attorney General A. Mitchell Palmer felt compelled to act. On January 2, 1920, agents of the Department of Justice arrested over 5,000 people across America. The Palmer Raids violated civil liberties by breaking into homes and union offices without arrest warrants. Although most of those arrested were released, the Department of Justice deported about 500 aliens without hearings or trials.

THE ROARING TWENTIES

1. The Palmer Raids marked the end of the Red Scare. However, they did not mark the end of intolerance and nativism. During the early 1920s, membership in the Ku Klux Klan swelled to as many as 4 million people. The revived Klan endorsed white supremacy and immigration restriction. Congress responded to this nativist pressure by passing the National Origins Act of 1924. The law established quotas that sharply reduced the flow of immigrants from Southern and Eastern Europe.

2. The Republican Party controlled the White House during the 1920s. Presidents Harding, Coolidge, and Hoover all rejected Wilson's vision of American leadership in the League of Nations. They also largely ignored the idealistic proposals of reform-minded Progressives. Instead, Harding began the decade by promising the nation an escape from complex problems and a return to "normalcy." For Harding, Coolidge, and Hoover, normalcy meant pursuing pro-business policies and avoiding troublesome domestic issues.

3. The 1920s witnessed the mass production of a new generation of affordable consumer products. Labor-saving devices such as refrigerators, washing

machines, electric irons, and vacuum cleaners made household chores easier, thus creating time to enjoy leisure activities.

4. The mass production of automobiles had the greatest impact upon American society. Surging car sales stimulated the growth of companies that produced steel, rubber, tires, glass, and gasoline. Within a few years, the automobile transformed America from a land of isolated farms and small towns into a nation of cities and suburbs connected by paved roads.

5. On November 2, 1920, radio station KDKA in Pittsburgh, Pennsylvania turned on its new transmitter and broadcast the news that American voters had elected Warren Harding as the nation's new president. KDKA's reign as America's only operating radio station did not last long. By the middle of the decade over 600 new stations broadcast a mix of news, weather forecasts, sports scores, popular music, comedy routines, and most of all commercials to an audience of 50 million listeners.

6. The radio boom and the mass production of automobiles and consumer goods fueled a spectacular economic boom. Materialism flourished as advertisements urged consumers to "buy now and pay later." During the period from 1921 to 1929, America's gross national product soared from $74 billion to $104.4 billion. The unprecedented prosperity seemed to promise a glittering future that would continue to offer endless enjoyment.

7. The GREAT MIGRATION of African Americans from the rural South to industrial cities in the North and Midwest continued during the 1920s. Harlem emerged as a vibrant center of African American culture. During the 1920s a new generation of black writers and artists created an outpouring of work known as the HARLEM RENAISSANCE. Many embraced the term "New Negro" as a proud assertion of their African American heritage and culture.

8. A group of writers and poets known as the Lost Generation became disillusioned with America's frivolous mass culture. Lost Generation writers such as Sinclair Lewis, F. Scott Fitzgerald, and T. S. Eliot criticized shallow middle-class materialism and mindless conformity.

9. The 1920s marked the appearance of America's first youth culture. A generation of under-25-year-olds deliberately flaunted new styles of dressing and new ways of behaving.

10. Young women known as FLAPPERS became the most publicized and controversial representatives of both rebellious youth and the new American woman. Flappers defied conventional standards by wearing short skirts and makeup, dancing to jazz, and enjoying wild parties. Print magazines,

Hollywood films, and radio advertisements all glamorized the flapper's carefree and often shocking lifestyle.

THE GREAT DEPRESSION

1. Farmers in the Midwest and South did not share in the good times of the 1920s. The global surplus of agricultural products drove prices and thus farm incomes down.

2. The United States economy was simultaneously experiencing overproduction by business and underconsumption by consumes. By the summer of 1929, many businesses had large inventories of unsold goods. Many factory workers lost their jobs as industries cut back production because of failing demand for their products.

3. Stock prices began to fall in September 1929. In late October they crashed, as stocks lost 37 percent of their value in just one week.

4. The stock market crash triggered a steep decline in industrial production. As more and more companies shut their doors, the unemployment rate sharply rose. By 1932, a quarter of all American workers had lost their jobs.

5. A severe drought hit the Great Plains starting in 1930. The lack of rain combined with unusually hot summers created great clouds of dust out of what had once been fertile soil. Large areas of Oklahoma, Kansas, and Colorado became known as the Dust Bowl.

6. During the 1930s, over 350,000 desperate people fled the Great Plains. John Steinbeck captured the ordeal of these so-called proud but impoverished Oakies in his powerful novel *The Grapes of Wrath*.

7. Dorothea Lange was a photographer whose poignant pictures publicized the plight of migrant farm workers and their families.

8. President Hoover did not support federal programs to aid unemployed workers. He believed the economy was basically sound and that recovery depended upon the support of the business community.

THE NEW DEAL

1. When Franklin D. Roosevelt took the oath of office on March 4, 1933, the United States faced a grave economic crisis. During the previous three years 86,000 businesses closed their doors, 9,000 banks declared bankruptcy, stocks lost 89 percent of their value, and the unemployment rate rose to a staggering 24.9 percent.

2. FDR promised and delivered a "New Deal for the American people." In just one hundred days, from March 9 to June 16, 1933, Congress approved fifteen major pieces of social and economic legislation.

3. Unlike either the Progressive era presidents or his predecessor Herbert Hoover, FDR recognized that America's millions of unemployed workers needed direct federal relief. For example, the Civilian Conservation Corp (CCC) created a jobs program for two million unemployed men aged 18 to 25. The men lived in camps and worked on a variety of conservation programs in the nation's parks and recreation areas.

4. The New Deal did more than provide immediate relief. It also attempted to promote economic recovery, institute long-term reforms, and restore public confidence in the nation's banking system. For example, the Glass-Steagall Banking Act established the Federal Deposit Insurance Corporation (FDIC) to guarantee bank deposits up to $5,000. The FDIC successfully calmed the public's fear of losing their hard-earned savings.

5. In 1934 and 1935 the Democratic majorities in Congress enacted a series of far-reaching programs known as the Second New Deal. The Social Security Act created a federal pension system funded by taxes on a worker's wages and by an equivalent contribution by employers. The Wagner Labor Relations Act recognized labor's right to bargain collectively. The new law created the National Labor Relations Board (NLRB) to protect workers from unfair practices and to arbitrate labor-management disputes.

6. The New Deal did not directly confront racial injustice. For example, CCC camps were often racially segregated. Nonetheless, the New Deal programs did create employment opportunities that helped African Americans survive the Great Depression. Despite the New Deal's limitations, African Americans overwhelmingly switched their allegiance from the Republican Party to FDR and the Democratic Party.

7. African American voters became an important part of the New Deal coalition of voters that formed during the 1930s. The coalition included urban Progressives, members of labor unions, ethnic minorities, and white Southerners. This coalition enabled the Democratic Party to win the White House in six of the eight presidential elections between 1936 and 1964.

8. New Deal programs were only partially successful in reducing unemployment and reviving the economy. The United States finally emerged from the Great Depression when the federal government sharply increased military spending at the beginning of the Second World War.

INTERWAR FOREIGN POLICY

1. In the years following the First World War, American ISOLATIONISTS argued that the United States should avoid entangling alliances with other countries. Instead, America pursued a unilateral foreign policy that emphasized international investments and peace treaties intended to safeguard national interests.

2. In 1933, FDR opened a new chapter in America's relationship with Latin America by proclaiming the beginning of a Good Neighbor Policy. The new policy renounced the Roosevelt Corollary and created reciprocal trade agreements between the United States and several Latin American countries. During the 1930s, the Good Neighbor Policy promoted a common hemispheric front against fascism.

3. During the 1930s, many Americans expressed concern about the rise of fascism in Italy and Germany. The march of fascist aggression persuaded America to rebuild the nation's military strength. However, a majority of the public still wanted to remain neutral.

4. Aware of the danger posed by Hitler's conquest of Poland and Western Europe, FDR announced that America would become an "arsenal of democracy" by providing additional war supplies to Great Britain and other nations fighting Nazi Germany. Under the Lend-Lease program, the United States supplied Great Britain, the Soviet Union, and other Allied nations with vast amounts of military equipment.

5. The war in Europe overshadowed ominous problems between the United States and Japan. Tensions between the two Pacific powers escalated when Japanese forces overran Indochina in July 1941. FDR retaliated by ordering a total embargo of oil and scrap iron shipments to Japan.

6. When negotiations with Japan reached an impasse, the Japanese launched a surprise attack on the American fleet stationed at Pearl Harbor. The attack on Pearl Harbor ended American neutrality. An angry and now united country entered the Second World War determined to crush Germany and Japan.

WWII: KEY HOMEFRONT DEVELOPMENTS

1. A wave of fear and suspicion swept across America in the weeks following the attack on Pearl Harbor. It was easy for frightened Americans to believe the West Coast would be Japan's next target. It was also easy to displace anger against Japan onto the approximately 110,000 people of Japanese birth and descent living on the West Coast.

2. On February 19, 1942, President Roosevelt responded to the public outcry by issuing an Executive Order authorizing the military to evacuate all people of Japanese ancestry to ten detention camps. In *Korematsu v. United States*, the Supreme Court upheld the constitutionality of the government's evacuation policy, citing the existence of "the gravest imminent danger to public safety." The Japanese internment is now recognized as the most serious violation of civil liberties in American history.

3. American factories used assembly-line techniques to mass-produce weapons, tanks, ships, and planes. The production miracle played a key role in defeating the Axis powers.

4. World War II created job opportunities for American women. The iconic "Rosie the Riveter" poster celebrated the women who worked in the nation's munitions factories.

5. Pressured by the threat of a protest march in Washington, D.C., FDR issued Executive Order 8802 providing for "the full and equitable participation of all workers in defense industries, without discrimination because of race, creed, or national origin." The order marked the first time since Reconstruction that the federal government committed itself to opposing racial discrimination.

6. African Americans were keenly aware of the contradiction between fighting for democracy abroad while endorsing racial discrimination at home. Black Americans enthusiastically supported a "Double V" campaign to win victory over fascism in Europe and victory over discrimination in the United States.

7. President Truman authorized the use of atomic bombs to devastate the Japanese cities of Hiroshima and Nagasaki. A variety of factors influenced his decision. First, Truman wanted to shock Japan into surrendering, thus saving lives of American soldiers preparing to invade the Japanese home islands. Second, he may also have been motivated by a desire to quickly end the war against Japan, thus deterring Soviet expansion in Asia. And finally, Truman may have wanted to convince Stalin of the need to be more cooperative in formulating postwar plans for Germany.

LOOKING IN-DEPTH
W.E.B. DU BOIS

In the introduction to his groundbreaking book, *The Souls of Black Folk*, W.E.B. DuBois predicted that "the problem of the twentieth century is the problem of the color line." Du Bois and most black leaders agreed that a combination of Jim Crow segregation, disenfranchisement, and lynching forced African Americans to accept a rigid color line that limited their economic opportunities and forced them to become second-class citizens. Although African American leaders agreed on the problems, they disagreed on the best strategy for confronting them.

In his famous "Atlanta Compromise Speech," Booker T. Washington cautioned Black Americans in the South to avoid political agitation and accept social segregation. Washington believed that black people were poor because they had few job skills. He therefore promoted industrial education as a necessary first step that would enable black people to learn useful trades and thus begin improving their lives.

Washington's conciliatory message pleased white leaders. However, younger educated African Americans led by Du Bois strongly criticized Washington's commitment to gradual progress. Du Bois charged that Washington's accommodationist strategy would only serve to perpetuate segregation and racial injustice. Instead, he advanced an alternate program of "ceaseless agitation" to challenge Jim Crow segregation and demand full economic, social, and political equality.

Du Bois understood that overcoming centuries of discrimination and racism would not be easy. He urged a "talented tenth" of educated black people to spearhead the fight for equal rights. In 1909, Du Bois and a number of prominent black and white reformers founded the National Association for the Advancement of Colored People (NAACP). The NAACP adopted a strategy of using lawsuits in federal courts to fight Jim Crow segregation.

So why should you remember W.E.B. Du Bois? Du Bois was a prolific author and an influential civil rights activist. He dedicated his life to ending the legal color line that deprived African Americans of their constitutional rights. Passed the year before his death, the Civil Rights Act of 1964 embodied many of the reforms for which Du Bois campaigned his entire life.

THE NEW IMMIGRANTS, 1890 – 1924

Have you or your family ever moved to a new town, city, or country? If so, then you know that moving can be a bewildering and frustrating experience. Being uprooted from your home means adjusting to a new environment, attending a new school, and finding a new job. Unlike most countries, the United States is predominately a nation of immigrants who experienced the trauma of moving.

Before 1890 most immigrants to the United States came from Western Europe and Scandinavia. However, the pattern of immigration began to dramatically change during the early 1890s as a new wave of immigrants began to arrive from Southern and Eastern European countries such as Italy, Poland, Russia, and Hungary. Between 1890 and 1920 over 16 million of these New Immigrants moved to America.

What factors caused this new wave of immigration? For some, the United States provided a refuge from the grinding poverty they had known at home. For others, it was a refuge from political oppression or religious persecution. Nearly all the immigrants believed that America was a land of opportunity where they could better themselves.

The overwhelming majority of the New Immigrants settled in large cities in the Northeast and Midwest. Most lived in crowded tenements and worked 12-hour days in grimy factories, dangerous coal mines, and dreary garment-making sweatshops.

The New Immigrants spoke a variety of languages and worked for low wages. Many were Roman Catholics and Jews at a time when America was overwhelmingly Protestant. Alarmed nativists accused the New Immigrants of being a threat to their jobs and way of life. One irate nativist expressed what many believed when he protested, "The scum of creation has been dumped on us."

So why should you remember the New Immigrants? The wave of New Immigrants provoked an anti-foreign reaction among native-born Protestants who clamored for laws that would severely restrict the flow of immigrants into the United States. During the early 1920s, Congress responded to public pressure by enacting a series of quota laws that sharply reduced the number of people who could immigrate to America.

MARCUS GARVEY

In May 1917, a 30-year-old black Jamaican named Marcus Garvey arrived in Harlem, the center of black cultural life in America. Garvey promptly organized a chapter of an organization he called the Universal Negro Improvement Association. Though hardly noticed at the time, Garvey's infant organization marked a milestone in the growth of black nationalism in the United States.

Garvey was a flamboyant and charismatic figure who was motivated by a powerful vision. Garvey rejected integration and instead preached a message of black pride and black self-help. He exhorted his followers to glorify their African heritage and rejoice in the beauty of their black skin. "We have a beautiful history," Garvey told his listeners, "and we shall create another one in the future."

Garvey's vision of black pride and black nationalism fueled the rapid growth of the Universal Negro Improvement Association. Within a short time, the UNIA became the first mass movement in African American history. By the mid-1920s, Garvey's organization had 700 branches in 38 states and the West Indies. The UNIA also published a newspaper with as many as 200,000 subscribers. By 1923, Garvey was one of the most famous black spokesmen in the world.

Garvey's fame proved to be short-lived. In the mid-1920s he was charged with mail fraud, jailed, and deported to his native Jamaica. Nonetheless, the man his followers called the "Black Moses" left behind a rich legacy. Dr. King captured the essence of Garvey's message of racial pride when he told an audience in Jamaica that Garvey, "was the first man of color to lead and develop a mass movement. He was the first man on a mass scale and level to give millions of Negroes a sense of dignity and destiny. And make the Negro feel he was somebody."

So why should you remember Marcus Garvey? APUSH test writers have begun to devote increased attention to Marcus Garvey. You should remember that Garvey rose to prominence during the 1920s as an advocate of black pride and black nationalism.

THE NEW DEAL COALITION

In 1928, American voters enthusiastically elected Herbert Hoover president of the United States. Hoover's election continued the era of Republican dominance that began with the election of McKinley in 1896. However, just four years later the Great Depression brought an abrupt end to Hoover's presidency. Led by Franklin D. Roosevelt, the revitalized Democratic Party enacted an ambitious program of relief, recovery, and reform known as the New Deal. The voting blocks and interest groups who supported FDR are known as the New Deal Coalition.

The New Deal Coalition included urban dwellers, labor unions, Catholics, Jews, white Southerners and African Americans. These voters formed a majority that enabled the Democratic Party to win the White House in six of the eight presidential elections between 1936 and 1964.

The presence of labor union members in the New Deal is not difficult to explain. Labor unions were among the primary beneficiaries of the New Deal. For example, the Wagner Act guaranteed workers the right to organize and bargain collectively.

The presence of white Southerners and African Americans in the same coalition requires a deeper historic analysis. Following Reconstruction, white-led Redeemer governments took power across the South. The whites were Democrats who shared an antipathy towards Republicans and black people. As you might expect, Black voters in the North formed a reliable Republican voting block. For example, in 1932, 75 percent of African American voters supported Herbert Hoover as the candidate of the party of Lincoln.

What caused the dramatic shift of African American voters to the Democratic Party? Although the New Deal did not oppose Jim Crow segregation, it did help African Americans survive the Great Depression. In the 1936 presidential election, 95 percent of black voters switched their allegiance to FDR and the Democratic Party. It is important to note that the alliance of Black voters and white Southern voters proved to be very fragile. As the Democratic Party began to actively support civil rights legislation in the 1950s and 1960s, its support among white Southerners began to steadily erode.

So why should you remember the New Deal coalition? APUSH test writers will expect you to know which voting blocks were in the New Deal coalition and which were not. Needless to say, small business leaders, industrialists, residents of small towns and suburbs were not part of the New Deal coalition. In addition, you should be aware that the 1936 election marked a historic shift of black voters to the Democratic Party.

THE JAPANESE INTERNMENT, 1942 – 1945

Revenge and fear can be a very dangerous and explosive combination of emotions. When the Japanese fleet struck Pearl Harbor on December 7, 1941, furious Americans demanded revenge. But revenge against Japan would have to wait for American factories to build a mighty armada of ships and planes. While American mobilized its forces, Guam, Hong Kong, Manila, and Singapore all fell to the seemingly invincible Imperial Japanese army.

As fear swept across America, it was easy to believe that the West Coast would be Japan's next target. It was also all too easy to displace anger and fear against Japan to the 110,000 people of Japanese birth and descent who lived in California.

From a purely objective point of view, Japanese Americans did not pose a security threat. They represented just one percent of the population of California and one tenth of one percent of the entire US population. However, panicked citizens and worried government officials viewed Japanese-Americans as traitors simply becauxe of their ancestry.

On February 19, 1942, President Roosevelt responded to the public outcry by signing Executive Order 9066 authorizing the military to evacuate all people of Japanese ancestry from the West Coast. The Japanese-Americans had just 48 hours to dispose of their businesses and property before reporting to Army-run Assembly Centers. In California alone, Japanese Americans lost nearly half a billion dollars in yearly income.

In a few months the War Relocation Authority moved the entire population of internees to desolate camps on federally owned property. No specific charges were ever filed against Japanese Americans and no evidence of subversion was ever found. The internment constituted the most serious violation of civil liberties in wartime in American history. In *Korematsu v. United States*, the Supreme Court upheld the constitutionality of the government's evacuation policy citing the existence of "the gravest imminent danger to public safety."

So why should you remember the Japanese internment? In the early months of World War II logic gave way to fear and panic. Like the Red Scare following

World War I, the Japanese internment provides a cautionary example of how war hysteria can led to frustration and a search for scapegoats.

CHAPTER 8
PERIOD 8
1945 – 1980

TIMELINE

1947	Truman Doctrine
1949	NATO established
1950	Korean War begins
1954	*Brown v. Board of Education*
1955	Montgomery Bus Boycott begins
1960	Sit-in protests begin
1962	Port Huron Statement
1963	March on Washington
1964	Civil Rights Act
1964	Gulf of Tonkin Resolution
1965	Great Society
1967	Summer of Love
1968	Martin Luther King Jr. assassinated
1969	Police raid Stonewall Inn
1970	First Earth Day
1972	Nixon travels to People's Republic of China
1973	Beginning of Arab oil embargo
1974	Nixon resigns
1978	Camp David Accords
1979	Americans taken hostage in Iran
1980	Ronald Reagan elected

THE COLD WAR, 1945 – 1953

1. The United States emerged from the Second World War as the world's foremost military, economic, and technological superpower. The Truman administration abandoned America's traditional isolationist policies and instead assumed the international responsibility of aiding democratic governments throughout the world.

2. The COLD WAR was a prolonged period of economic and political rivalry between the United States and the Soviet Union. It began with the announcement of the Truman Doctrine in 1947 and ended with the fall of the Berlin Wall in 1989 and the collapse of the Soviet Union in 1991.

3. CONTAINMENT was America's Cold War strategy of blocking the expansion of Soviet influence.

4. COLLECTIVE SECURITY is a principle of mutual support in which all nations in an alliance pledge to consider an attack on one as an attack on all.

5. The Truman Doctrine committed the United States to use its military and economic strength to block Soviet ideological influence and military power by supporting "free peoples" in Greece, Turkey, and Europe.

6. The Marshall Plan committed the United States to provide a massive program of economic assistance to help the nations of Western Europe recover from the devastation caused by the Second World War.

7. The Berlin Blockade marked the first great Cold War test of containment. The Berlin Airlift successfully thwarted the Soviet attempt to cut off supplies to West Berlin.

8. The United States, Canada, and ten Western European nations formed the NATO Alliance as an international security system to block Soviet expansion. The alliance operates on the principle of collective security.

9. Historian John Lewis Gaddis argues that the Cold War emerged from an "interactive system" in which the actions and responses of the United States and the Soviet Union produced an escalating spiral of mutual distrust and antagonism. For example, the Soviet Union's Berlin Blockade prompted the Berlin Airlift. These actions helped convince the United States and its allies to form the NATO Alliance. The Soviet Union then responded by forming the Warsaw Pact.

10. North Korea's surprise invasion of South Korea precipitated the Korean War. President Truman did not want to be accused of "losing" South Korea. He did not ask Congress for a declaration of war. Instead, American troops fought under the auspices of the United Nations.

THE RED SCARE AND MCCARTHYISM

1. The Communist victory in China and the outbreak of the Korean War shocked America. Public apprehension deepened when the Soviet Union exploded an atomic bomb, thus ending America's nuclear monopoly.

2. These stunning reversals heightened the public's fear that Communist agents had infiltrated the State Department and other sensitive government agencies.

3. Concern with internal security became more intense as Cold War tensions increased. The House Un-American Activities Committee (HUAC) soon began a major investigation of Communist subversives within the United States.

4. Prodded by the relentless investigations of Richard Nixon, HUAC discovered that a prominent State Department official named Alger Hiss had been a Soviet spy in the 1930s.

5. The Red Scare even extended to Hollywood. Motion picture executives drew up a "blacklist" of about 500 writers, directors, and actors who were suspended from work for their alleged support of left-wing political beliefs and associations.

6. Joseph McCarthy, a previously obscure senator from Wisconsin, skillfully exploited the political climate of anxiety and fear engendered by the Red Scare. McCarthy's practice of making unsubstantiated accusations of disloyalty without evidence became known as McCARTHYISM. His campaign of innuendo and half-truths made him one of the most feared and powerful politicians in America.

7. McCarthy finally caused his own downfall when he launched a televised investigation of the U.S. Army. A national audience of more than 20 million people watched as McCarthy bullied witnesses, twisted people's testimonies, and used phony evidence. The Army-McCarthy hearings swiftly turned public sentiment against McCarthy.

THE 1950S: PROSPERITY AND CONFORMITY

1. The fall of McCarthyism corresponded with a period of unprecedented prosperity. The gross national product soared from $200 billion in 1945 to $500 billion in 1960. With just six percent of the world's population, Americans drove 75 percent of the world's automobiles, consumed half of its energy, and produced almost half of its manufactured products.

2. America's robust economic growth sparked a strong demand for new homes in the suburbs. New interstate highways enabled suburbanites to commute from their homes to jobs in the cities.

3. Much of the suburban growth occurred in the SUNBELT, an arc of states stretching from the Carolinas to Florida and on to Texas and Southern California. Unprecedented prosperity enabled millions of middle-class Americans to migrate from declining industrial cities in the North to Sunbelt cities and suburbs that featured air-conditioning and low taxes. As its population grew, the Sunbelt steadily gained political, economic, and cultural influence.

4. On January 19, 1953, a record audience turned on over 70 percent of America's television sets to watch an episode of I Love Lucy featuring the birth of Lucy's son, Little Ricky. The overwhelming popularity of this program provided a vivid example of the explosive growth of television. In 1946 there were just 7,000 TV sets and six TV stations in the entire country. By 1953 half of all homes had a TV set and the average family spent five hours a day gathered around it. Like radio in the 1920s, television played an increasingly important role in shaping public opinion and stimulating consumer demand for new products.

5. Economic prosperity and suburban growth did not encourage a renewal of women's rights activism. Instead magazines, movies, and television programs all glamorized romantic love and celebrated marriage.

6. The marriage boom triggered a postwar BABY BOOM. The 1950s witnessed a tidal wave of 40 million births. The young families populated suburbs that became known for a revival of the CULT OF DOMESTICITY. The mass media reinforced and idealized traditional gender roles in which men commuted to work while their wives stayed home and raised their children.

7. Not all Americans hailed the rapid suburbanization of American life. In her song "Little Boxes," Malvina Reynolds decried the homogenized suburbs where everyone lived in "little boxes" that "all look just the same." A group of writers and poets known as BEATS shared Reynold's disdain for middle-class culture. Like the Lost Generation of the 1920s, Beat writers felt alienated from America's excessive materialism and constant pressure to get along.

THE CIVIL RIGHTS MOVEMENT, 1954 – 1963

1. The Supreme Court ruling in *Brown v. Board of Education of Topeka* overturned the "separate but equal" doctrine established in *Plessy v. Ferguson.* The Court ruled that racial segregation in public schools was

a denial of the equal protection of laws guaranteed by the Fourteenth Amendment. The decision reflected the growing belief after the Second World War that the power of the federal government should be used to promote greater racial justice.

2. The unanimous *Brown* decision opened a new era in the African American struggle for equal rights by placing the Supreme Court on the side of racial justice. Galvanized by the Court's ruling, America's 15 million black citizens began to demand "Freedom Now!"

3. Southern segregationists called for "massive resistance" to the *Brown* decision. The Little Rock school crisis marked a major test of the federal government's willingness to enforce the Supreme Court's order to desegregate public schools "with all deliberate speed."

4. The next step on the road to freedom began on a bus in Montgomery, Alabama. On December 1, 1955, a weary black seamstress named Rosa Parks defied local segregation laws and refused to give up her bus seat to a white man. Her arrest outraged Park's 26-year-old minister, Dr. Martin Luther King, Jr.

5. Dr. King mobilized Montgomery's black community by organizing a boycott of the city buses. His leadership in the Montgomery Bus Boycott transformed him from an unknown local minister into America's foremost civil rights leader. Within a short time, Dr. King founded the Southern Christian Leadership Council (SCLC) to apply the principles of nonviolent civil disobedience to test cases across the South.

6. The victories in Montgomery and Little Rock did not end segregation's iron grip on Southern life. Dr. King's philosophy of nonviolent civil disobedience inspired four black college students in Greensboro, North Carolina to take action. Calling segregation "evil, pure and simple," the Greensboro Four sat down at a "whites only" Woolworth lunch counter and ordered coffee and apple pie. When the waitress refused to take their order, the students remained seated. Their "sit-in" tactic worked; six months later the Greensboro Woolworth desegregated its lunch counter.

7. The Greensboro sit-ins energized student-led protests across the South. A growing wave of student protesters held "read-ins" at libraries, "watch-ins" at movie theatres, and "wade-ins" at beaches.

8. The March on Washington was a massive demonstration to build a "coalition of conscience" to support President Kennedy's civil rights bill.

THE GREAT SOCIETY

1. President Lyndon B. Johnson plunged into his presidential duties in the dark days following the assassination of President Kennedy. In May 1964 he delivered a speech challenging America to build a "Great Society" that would use the power of the federal government to end racial segregation, fight poverty, and promote social welfare.

2. LBJ understood that the fight against Jim Crow segregation posed the nation's most urgent social problem. He proudly signed the landmark 1964 Civil Rights Act into law on July 2, 1964. The act barred discrimination in public facilities such as hotels, restaurants, and theaters. The legislation authorized the attorney general to bring suits to accelerate school desegregation. In addition, the act outlawed discrimination in employment on the basis of race, religion, national origin, or sex.

3. President Johnson and civil rights leaders next turned to the issue of voting rights. The Fifteenth Amendment gave black males the right to vote. However, a combination of literacy tests and poll taxes effectively nullified the amendment. The Voting Rights Act of 1965 made the Fifteenth Amendment an operative part of the Constitution. The law ended literacy tests and other devices used to prevent African Americans from voting.

4. President Johnson believed his landslide victory in the 1964 presidential election gave him a mandate to pursue his dream of waging an "unconditional War on Poverty." Congress supported the President's bold initiative by passing a host of new federal programs to help the poor. For example, high school dropouts learned new skills in over fifty Job Corps camps.

5. The Great Society also dealt with the pressing health care needs of America's senior citizens. The Social Security Amendments of 1965 created Medicare and Medicaid. These programs established government health insurance coverage for elderly and poor Americans.

6. The Immigration Act of 1965 abolished the system of national quotas enacted by the National Origins Act of 1924. Although it was not recognized at the time, the new law had the unintended consequence of permitting a new wave of immigration from Latin America and Asia.

7. The Great Society did not ignore the environment. For example, the Water Quality Act of 1965 set national standards for water quality.

THE VIETNAM WAR

1. France conquered Vietnam during the late 1800s. By the 1930s, Vietnam became a prized colonial possession that produced all of France's raw

rubber and much of its imported rice. Following the Second World War, communist forces led by Ho Chi Minh declared Vietnam an independent country. However, the French refused to accept the loss of their valuable colony. Supported by generous American aid, the French soon became entangled in a costly war with Ho's guerilla forces. The war ended in a disastrous French defeat that left Vietnam divided at the 17th parallel. Ho Chi Minh and his communist government ruled north of the parallel, while a French-backed government ruled south of the parallel.

2. The French defeat forced President Eisenhower to make a crucial decision. The U.S. experience in Korea seemed to validate the belief that American power could be effectively used to contain Communism in Asia. Ike refused to abandon Vietnam. According to the widely accepted DOMINO THEORY, the fall of South Vietnam would inevitably lead to Communist expansion throughout the rest of Southeast Asia.

3. During his inaugural address, President Kennedy pledged the United States would "pay any price, bear any burden, meet any hardship…to assure the survival and the success of liberty." At the time he made this pledge, South Vietnamese communists called Viet Cong began to fight a guerilla war to overthrow the American-backed government. Kennedy responded by ordering over 16,000 American military advisors to help train the South Vietnamese army.

4. President Johnson inherited a dangerously deteriorating situation in South Vietnam. Bombings by Viet Cong terrorists became an almost daily occurrence as rural roads became death traps for government soldiers. Sensing that South Vietnam was on the verge of collapse, the North Vietnamese sent more aid to reinforce the Viet Cong.

5. On August 4, 1964, President Johnson received unsubstantiated reports that North Vietnamese gunboats had fired on two American destroyers patrolling the Gulf of Tonkin. The next day, Johnson asked Congress to pass a resolution authorizing him to take "all necessary measures to repel any armed attacks against the forces of the United States and to prevent further aggression." Passed with almost-unanimous Congressional support, the Gulf of Tonkin Resolution gave President Johnson a blank check to escalate the American war effort in Vietnam.

6. In March 1965, President Johnson took the fateful step of ordering a massive escalation of U.S. forces in Vietnam. However, the Viet Cong's refusal to fight large-scale battles turned the war into an endless series of small but terrifying clashes. Still convinced that American power would prevail, Johnson poured additional men and money into the war effort. By the end

of 1967, almost 500,000 American soldiers guarded South Vietnam's cities and towns.

7. When the war did not end quickly, a growing number of alarmed citizens began to question America's involvement in Vietnam. By the end of 1967, the war polarized Americans into "hawks" who supported the war effort and "doves" who opposed it. The high cost of the war crippled Johnson's Great Society programs and eroded his popularity.

8. On January 31, 1968, Viet Cong and North Vietnamese forces launched a surprise attack on over one hundred cities, villages, and military bases across South Vietnam. The Tet Offensive marked a turning point in the Vietnam War. Although U.S. forces regained the initiative and won a military victory, the heavy fighting undermined Johnson's confident prediction that "victory was just around the corner." Faced with plummeting public approval, Johnson told a nationally televised audience that he would not seek reelection.

9. Richard Nixon won the presidency in 1968 with a promise to achieve "peace with honor" in Vietnam. He announced a policy called VIETNAMIZATION that called for the training of South Vietnamese soldiers to take the place of withdrawing American forces.

10. After five more years of bloody fighting and intense U.S. bombing, Nixon signed an agreement that called for the release of American prisoners of war and the withdrawal of the remaining U.S. troops and advisors.

11. The Vietnam War ended in 1975 when the North Vietnamese captured Saigon and unified all of Vietnam. Unlike the armistice that ended fighting in Korea, the fall of Saigon resulted in a defeat for the United States policy of containment.

YOUTH CULTURE OF THE 1960S

1. Conformity and consensus dominated American life during the 1950s. The nation's thriving economy supported look-alike suburbs that encouraged consumerism and a revival of the cult of domesticity. A silent generation of college students accepted America's anti-communist foreign policy and the racial status quo in the South.

2. The civil rights sit-ins and protest marches signaled the end of the apathy that had blanketed college campuses. In 1962, members of the Students for a Democratic Society (SDS) issued the Port Huron Statement, expressing their growing concern about "events too troubling to dismiss." The

"troubling" events included social inequities exposed by the Civil Rights movement and disillusionment with America's overly materialistic culture.

3. The SDS and other New Left groups rejected traditional liberal policies. They argued that political leaders were doing too little to address America's racial and economic status quo.

4. Inspired by civil rights protests and mobilized by the Vietnam War, a youthful rebellion burst across America during the second half of the 1960s. Called hippies, a growing number of young people challenged traditional values by offering an alternative lifestyle or COUNTERCULTURE.

5. Hippies rejected the values of hard work, neat appearance, and economic competition taught by their parents. Instead, the counterculture stressed the importance of personal liberation by being "groovy" and "doing your own thing." Hippies believed they were leading America into a new age of harmony and understanding.

6. The counterculture did not dismantle the political establishment or the capitalist economic system. However, the movement's tolerant view of sexual roles helped pave the way for the 1970s women's liberation movement. In addition, the counterculture's disdain for the repressive norms of mainstream culture helped inspire previously marginalized people such as gays and lesbians to launch enduring rights movements.

7. The counterculture shocked and offended Americans who upheld the nation's traditional values. These Americans became part of a cultural and political backlash that rejuvenated the conservative movement, sparked the rise of the "moral majority," and played a key role in the election of Ronald Reagan in 1980.

BLACK POWER AND A NEW MILITANCY

1. The Civil Rights Act of 1964 and the Voting Rights Act of 1965 represent historic achievements that struck down Jim Crow segregation. However, these legislative victories did not satisfy a new generation of black leaders living in urban ghettos. They pointed to decaying cities, soaring crime rates, and depression-level unemployment as evidence of problems that could not be solved by sit-ins and freedom marches.

2. Malcolm X emerged as a charismatic black leader who demanded radical change. He rejected Dr. King's strategy of nonviolence and vision of a racially integrated society. Instead, Malcolm X advocated black separatism, black pride, and the expansion of links with the newly independent nations in Africa.

3. Malcolm X became America's most effective militant voice. However, on February 21, 1965, assassins suddenly unleashed a barrage of bullets, silencing the most articulate spokesman for black militants since Marcus Garvey.

4. Stokely Carmichael soon replaced Malcolm X as America's most militant black leader. Carmichael and other advocates of BLACK POWER argued that African Americans should build economic and political power by forming black-owned businesses and voting for black candidates for political offices.

5. The Civil Rights movement raised high hopes that could not be quickly fulfilled. At the same time, the Black Power movement inflamed long-simmering tensions in inner cities across America. Beginning in 1965, long hot summers brought civil unrest that scarred hundreds of urban areas across America.

6. The mounting civil unrest alarmed the nation and prompted President Johnson to appoint a special commission to investigate the causes of the riots. The Kerner Commission concluded that the migration of middle-class families to suburbs left inner-city neighborhoods impoverished. The commission warned, "Our nation is moving toward two societies, one black one white – separate and unequal."

7. The Black Power movement forced Dr. King to expand his focus from civil rights to the deep-rooted problems caused by inner-city poverty. At the same time, he became an outspoken critic of the Vietnam War.

8. Determined to promote economic justice, Dr. King traveled to Memphis to support a strike by the city's underpaid sanitation workers. On the evening of April 4, 1968, a white assassin later identified as James Earl Ray, fired a high-powered bullet that struck and killed Dr. King as he stood on a motel balcony. The tragic news sparked a wave of rioting that impacted over 130 cities.

9. Dr. King left an enduring legacy that transformed American society. In just over a decade he led a campaign of nonviolent protests, dismantling a system of segregation that had stood essentially unchanged since Reconstruction. His famous dream of a just society continues to inspire Americans to work for a future without racial prejudice and discrimination.

THE CIVIL RIGHTS MOVEMENT EXPANDS

1. The Civil Rights movement created a climate of protest that inspired other discontented minority groups. During the late 1960s and throughout

the 1970s, Native Americans, Hispanics, and gays all formed movements demanding that America address their grievances.

2. In 1968, a group of young, militant Native Americans embraced the concept of "Red Power" by forming the American Indian Movement (AIM). Inspired by the Black Power movement, AIM activists staged well-publicized protests at Alcatraz Island in San Francisco Bay and at the village of Wounded Knee in South Dakota.

3. The Red Power movement fostered a growing sense of pan-Indian identity. Their protests helped mobilize public support for the Indian Education Act of 1972 which provided federal funds for school districts with a high percentage of indigenous children.

4. Like their Native American and African American counterparts, young Mexican Americans became more militant. For example, Cesar Chavez and Dolores Huerta co-founded the United Farm Workers (UFW) to represent thousands of vineyard workers. Inspired by Dr. King's nonviolent tactics, Chavez staged a 28-day hunger strike, led peaceful protest marches, and appealed for a nationwide boycott of grapes. Pressured by a boycott that grew to include 17 million consumers, growers signed a contract recognizing the UFW.

5. During the 1960s, most states defined homosexuality as an immoral and illegal activity. Police used vice laws to harass and arrest gay men and lesbians.

6. The Stonewall Inn was a popular gay bar in New York City's Greenwich Village. Police officers raided the inn during the early morning hours of June 28, 1969. The raids provoked spontaneous demonstrations calling for an end to police harassment.

7. The Stonewall Riots played a key role in sparking the modern Gay Liberation movement. By 1973, there were about 800 gay organizations across America.

THE ENVIRONMENTAL MOVEMENT

1. In just one generation, the American people moved from the depths of the Great Depression to enjoy the highest standard of living the world had ever known. However, the unparalleled growth came with an environmental price. In 1959, industrial and private sources of pollution emitted 24.9 million tons of soot into the air. Frequent smog alerts became a worrying part of daily life in Los Angeles, New York City, and other metropolitan centers across America.

2. Chemical companies hailed DDT as a miracle synthetic pesticide that would eradicate mosquitoes and other harmful insect pests. However, an American marine biologist named Rachel Carson conducted research indicating that DDT and other chemicals were in fact killing beneficial insects, bees, livestock, and birds. Carson published her findings in *Silent Spring*, a groundbreaking book that helped launch an environmental movement based upon the ecological principle that all life is part of an integrated web.

3. In January 1969 an oil rig explosion in the Santa Barbara Channel turned miles of pristine Southern California beaches into an environmental nightmare. Within days, a black tide 6 inches thick covered 800 miles of ocean and 35 miles of coast.

4. Just six months later, a second environmental disaster struck the Cuyahoga River in Cleveland, Ohio. For years, steel mills, oil refineries, chemical companies, and local residents dumped waste including raw sewage, acid, and floating debris into the river. On June 22, 1969, sparks from a train ignited a fire that damaged two bridges. Pictures of a river on fire became a symbol of environmental degradation.

5. The Santa Barbara oil spill and the Cuyahoga River fire appalled the public and helped spur widespread protests. On April 22, 1970, over 20 million concerned citizens participated in America's first annual Earth Day. Fully 70 percent of the public ranked the environment as the nation's most pressing problem.

6. Congress responded to the public outcry by enacting a far-reaching program of environmental legislation. The Clean Air Act set stricter standards to reduce automobile and factory emissions. The Water Pollution Control Act provided funds to protect America's sea coasts and clean up its neglected rivers and lakes. The Endangered Species Act protected rare plants and animals from extinction. In addition to these measures, the Nixon administration banned the use of DDT and created the Environmental Protection Agency (EPA) to enforce a range of environmental guidelines.

THE 1970S – POLITICAL SCANDALS, ECONOMIC CHALLENGES, AND FOREIGN POLICY CRISES

1. As the leader of the free world, the United States attempted to contain Soviet expansion and isolate the People's Republic of China. President Nixon believed the time had come to pursue bold policy initiatives that would reshape global politics.

2. In February 1972, Nixon became the first American president to visit the People's Republic of China. His historic trip opened a new era of cultural exchanges and trade between the two countries.

3. Three months after returning from China, Nixon again stunned the world by becoming the first American president to visit Moscow. During the seven-day summit, Nixon and Soviet Premier Leonid Brezhnev signed a Strategic Arms Limitation Treaty (SALT) that placed limits on both the number of intercontinental ballistic missiles and the construction of antiballistic missile systems.

4. The SALT I treaty signaled the beginning of a new period of DÉTENTE, or relaxed tensions, between the two Cold War rivals.

5. In October 1973, Egypt and Syria attacked Israel on Yom Kippur, the holiest day of the Jewish year. Although American military aid enabled Israel to prevail, the effects of the Yom Kippur War continued.

6. Nixon's decision to help Israel angered many oil-rich Arab nations. As the most important members of the Organization of Petroleum Exporting Countries (OPEC), they had the power to reduce the supply of oil and raise prices. On October 20, 1973, they chose to do both.

7. The Arab oil embargo quickly disrupted daily life in the United States. Motorists who had assumed that gasoline would always be cheap and plentiful found themselves waiting in lines up to two miles long to buy fuel that had nearly doubled in price.

8. The effects of the energy crisis did not end with the lifting of the embargo in April 1974. The oil embargo marked the end of the post-World War II economic boom and the beginning of an inflationary spiral that plagued the U.S. economy during the rest of the 1970s.

9. On June 17, 1972, police arrested five burglars who had broken into the headquarters of the Democratic National Committee at the Watergate apartment and office complex in Washington, DC.

10. President Nixon was never directly implicated in the Watergate break-in. However, instead of firing the corrupt officials responsible for the crime, he chose to "play it tough" and attempt to cover-up the scandal.

11. The House Judiciary Committee ultimately voted to recommend that Nixon be impeached for obstruction of justice. On August 9, 1974, Richard Nixon became the first president to resign from office. Vice-President Gerald Ford then became the nation's 38th president.

12. A month after Nixon's resignation, Ford surprised the nation by granting the former president a full pardon. Although unpopular, the pardon did

help put aside the Watergate issue. Meanwhile, soaring inflation and rising unemployment damaged Ford's popularity. His inability to revive the economy enabled the Democratic candidate, Jimmy Carter, to win the 1976 presidential election.

13.   Carter faced a seemingly intractable economic problem. The American economy was simultaneously experiencing a combination of rising unemployment and double-digit inflation. Economists called this unusual phenomenon STAGFLATION.

14.   President Carter's commitment to patient negotiation achieved a dramatic breakthrough in Middle East diplomacy. The Camp David accords ended 30 years of intermittent war and hostility between Egypt and Israel.

15.   The Camp David Accords marked Carter's greatest triumph. But just over a year later, an Iranian mob stormed the U.S. embassy in Tehran and took more than 50 Americans hostage. The hostage crisis plunged the Carter presidency into a diplomatic dilemma it was unable to successfully resolve.

16.   The Iranian hostage crisis, double-digit inflation, and a continued rise in energy prices seriously weakened Carter's popularity and led to Ronald Reagan's victory in the 1980 presidential election.

LOOKING IN-DEPTH
THE TRUMAN DOCTRINE, 1947

What do you think was the most important post-World War II speech in American history? Dr. King's "I Have a Dream" speech, President Kennedy's Inaugural Address, and President Reagan's "Evil Empire" speech would no doubt all receive support from APUSH students. However, foreign policy experts would disagree. They argue that President Truman's address to a joint session of Congress on March 12, 1947, was what the eminent Cold War historian John Spanier calls "one of the most important speeches in American history."

Truman began his speech by explaining that Soviet pressure threatened the independence of Greece. "If Greece should fall under the control of an armed minority," he gravely concluded, "the effect upon Turkey would be immediate and serious." The President then asked Congress to appropriate $400 million for economic and military supplies for Greece and Turkey.

Truman did not stop with a request for money. The United States, he declared, could survive only in a world in which freedom flourished. He then articulated what became known as the Truman Doctrine: "I believe that it must be the policy of the United States to support free peoples who are resisting attempted subjugations by armed minorities or by outside pressures."

Congress promptly approved Truman's request for economic aid to help Greece and Turkey resist Communist influence. The Truman Doctrine thus marked the beginning of the Cold War between the United States and the Soviet Union. As the leader of the Free World, America pledged to use its strength to contain or limit the spread of Communism throughout the world. This commitment dominated American foreign policy from 1947 to the collapse of the Soviet Union in 1991.

So why should you remember the Truman Doctrine? The Truman Doctrine has generated a significant cluster of APUSH multiple-choice and free-response questions. It is very important that you know that the Truman Doctrine embodies the principles of containment first articulated by George Kennan. You should also know that the Truman Doctrine was first applied to Greece and Turkey.

McCARTHYISM, 1950 – 1954

On the morning of February 9, 1950, Joseph R. McCarthy was an obscure Republican Senator from Wisconsin. But that night everything suddenly changed when he boldly told an audience in Wheeling, West Virginia, "I have in my hand a list of 205 names known to the Secretary of State as being members of the Communist Party and who nevertheless are still working and shaping the policy of the State Department." In speeches given the following days, McCarthy repeated his charges but changed the number of names on his list from 205 "security risks" to "57 card-carrying Communists."

McCarthy's accusations did not go unnoticed. Although never substantiated, his claims touched a particularly sensitive public nerve. In the four years since the end of World War II, the Soviet Union changed from an ally to a mortal threat to the American way of life. Led by Joseph Stalin, the Soviet Union dominated Eastern Europe, threatened West Berlin, and exploded an atomic bomb. Angry and bewildered Americans demanded to know what had gone wrong.

Senator McCarthy skillfully exploited the political climate of paranoia. Millions of people listened as McCarthy branded Secretary of State Dean Acheson "the Red Dean" and thundered that America was being sold out by "bright young men who are born with silver spoons in their mouths." But McCarthyism involved more than calling people names. Government agencies demanded loyalty oaths and Hollywood studios blacklisted hundreds of actors, screenwriters, directors, and even makeup artists who were suspected of having Communist affiliations.

McCarthy finally caused his own downfall when he launched a televised investigation of the U.S. Army. He bullied witnesses, twisted people's testimonies, and used phony evidence. Finally, Army counsel Joseph Welsh castigated McCarthy for his "reckless and cruel" accusations. He then pointedly asked McCarthy, "Have you no sense of decency?" Suddenly dumbfounded, McCarthy squirmed in his seat and asked, "What did I do?"

The Army-McCarthy hearings swiftly turned public sentiment against McCarthy. In December 1954 the full Senate formally censured McCarthy for his dishonorable conduct. Flashing his famous grin, President Eisenhower asked his cabinet, "Have you heard the latest? McCarthyism is McCarthywasm."

So why should you remember McCarthyism? The brief but intense outburst of McCarthyism formed an important part of the Red Scare during the early 1950s. McCarthy's accusations reflected the public's growing anxiety about Soviet influence at home and abroad. The McCarthy era had many characteristics in common with the attacks on radicals and immigrants following the First World War.

BROWN V. BOARD OF EDUCATION, 1954

On May 17, 1954, a hushed audience of reporters closely watched as all nine Supreme Court justices solemnly entered the Court's ornate chamber. Americans, and indeed people all over the world, waited anxiously to hear the Court's decision in the case of *Brown v. Board of Education of Topeka*. The wait soon ended. Chief Justice Earl Warren firmly announced the Court's unanimous decision: "We conclude that in the field of public education the doctrine of separate but equal has no place. Separate educational facilities are inherently unequal."

The Court's momentous decision had deep roots in America's long and complicated history of race relations. In 1868, the states ratified the Fourteenth Amendment. It declared that "No state shall deny to any person within its jurisdiction the equal protection of the laws." However, in the 1890s Southern states began to enact laws segregating railroads and streetcars. In 1896 the Supreme Court ruled in *Plessy v. Ferguson* that "separate but equal" facilities are constitutional. Segregation soon became a pervasive part of life in the South. By 1954, seventeen Southern states and the District of Columbia mandated segregated public schools for black and white children.

In his famous dissent to *Plessy v. Ferguson*, Justice Harlan asserted that "our Constitution is color-blind." By reversing *Plessy v. Ferguson*, the Warren Court enlarged the concept of equality by declaring that "all classification by race is unconstitutional." The Brown decision thus opened a new era in the African American struggle for equal rights. In 1955 the Supreme Court unanimously directed the states to desegregate their public schools with "all deliberate speed." Led by Dr. King and other civil rights activists, more than 15 million black citizens began to demand "Freedom Now!"

So why should you remember *Brown v. Board of Education of Topeka*? Needless to say, the Brown decision has generated a significant number of APUSH questions. You should be able to recognize a quote from Chief Justice Warren's famous ruling and of course know that the Brown decision reversed *Plessy v. Ferguson*. It is also important to be familiar with President Eisenhower's decision to send federal troops to Little Rock, Arkansas, to enforce the Court's desegregation order.

THE GULF OF TONKIN RESOLUTION, 1964

Let me ask you a question: Is it possible for an event that didn't occur to have major historic consequences and become a frequently tested event on the APUSH exam? Surprisingly, the answer is yes! Let me explain:

In early August 1964, US Navy warships were cooperating with South Vietnamese gunboats in provocative raids along the coast of North Vietnam. On August 4th, two of these American destroyers reported that they were being attacked by North Vietnamese torpedo boats. However, the commander of one of the ships soon radioed that there had been no actual "visual sighting" of the enemy ships. The reported contact may have been due to "freak weather" conditions which affected the ship's sonar and radar.

Although what actually happened was unclear, President Johnson told a nationally televised audience that "hostile actions against United States ships" had forced him to respond to North Vietnamese aggression. Even as he spoke, 64 US jets roared across the Gulf of Tonkin and then bombed North Vietnamese naval bases.

The next day Johnson asked Congress to pass a resolution authorizing him to take "all necessary measures to repel any armed attack against the forces of the United States and to prevent further aggression." Congress and the American public were not told about the secret raids on North Vietnam or the new evidence that an attack may not have occurred. Unaware of this information, the House unanimously supported the Gulf of Tonkin Resolution while only two Senators opposed it.

Johnson's handling of the Gulf of Tonkin affair seemed to be a major political success. The Tonkin Gulf Resolution sent a clear signal to North Vietnam that America would defend South Vietnam. Opinion polls showed that 72 percent of the public supported LBJ's handling of the war in Vietnam. Very few people listened when Senator Wayne Morse, who voted against the resolution, warned: "We are in effect giving the President warmaking powers in the absence of a declaration of war. I believe that to be a historic mistake."

So why should you remember the Gulf of Tonkin Resolution? Make sure that you remember that the resolution gave President Johnson a blank check to escalate the Vietnam War. Congress thus surrendered its war-making power to the President.

THE GREAT SOCIETY, 1965

I'd like to begin by asking you to think outside the box. Let's pretend that the voters have just elected you President of the United States. Your landslide victory includes two-thirds majorities in both houses of Congress. How would you use your political mandate? What vision would you have for America?

As 1965 began, President Lyndon Baines Johnson faced this exact same situation. His overwhelming victory in the 1964 election gave him an opportunity to build what LBJ called "the Great Society." Johnson eloquently summarized his vision for the Great Society when he told Congress: "I do not want to be the President who built empires…I want to be the President who educated young children… who helped to feed the hungry…who helped the poor to find their way…"

Like the New Deal programs, the Great Society proposed to use the power of the federal government to fight poverty and unemployment. In a widely read book entitled *The Other America*, the social critic Michael Harrington argued that about one-fifth of the nation's families were mired in what he called "a culture of poverty." Shocked by Harrington's compelling anecdotes and statistical evidence, LBJ declared an "unconditional War on Poverty."

The Great Society also included far-reaching legislation designed to address a number of pressing problems. The Voting Rights Act of 1965 abolished literacy tests and enforced the voting rights of African Americans. The Immigration Act of 1965 abolished the system of quotas instituted by the National Origins Act of 1924. The Social Security Amendment of 1965 created Medicare and Medicaid, providing health insurance coverage for elderly and poor Americans. And finally, the Elementary and Secondary Education Act of 1965 provided over one billion dollars in federal aid to help school systems purchase textbooks and new library materials.

So why should you remember the Great Society? APUSH test writers expect you to know which programs were included in the Great Society and which were not. For example, the Peace Corps and guaranteed employment were NOT part of the Great Society. It is also important to be able to compare and contrast the Great Society with the New Deal. Both programs used the federal government to promote social change. However, unlike the New Deal, the Great Society included significant legislation to protect the civil liberties and voting rights of African Americans.

CHAPTER 9
PERIOD 9
1980 – 2010

TIMELINE

1980   Ronald Reagan elected

1989   Fall of the Berlin Wall

1991   Collapse of the Soviet Union

2001   *9/11 attacks*

2001   USA Patriot Act

2007   First iPhone

THE CONSERVATIVE RESURGENCE

1. The SUNBELT comprised a booming region of 14 states stretching from North Carolina through Florida and Texas to Arizona and California. These states experienced unprecedented growth during the 1970s.

2. The prosperous suburbs surrounding Los Angeles, Phoenix, Dallas, and Atlanta quickly became conservative strongholds. White, middle-class suburbanites embraced a conservative philosophy favoring reductions in expensive government welfare programs and burdensome business regulations.

3. The 1960s and 1970s produced a number of social and cultural challenges that alarmed Christian evangelicals. Sexual permissiveness, the Equal Rights Amendment, and legalized abortion galvanized a determined group of conservative Christians known as the Religious Right.

4. Beginning with the New Deal, working-class voters formed a core group in the Democratic Party coalition. However, by the late 1970s, slowing wage growth, rising prices, and growing tax burdens prompted many of these voters to rethink their loyalty to the Democratic Party.

5. During the fall of 1980, millions of concerned Americans felt squeezed by double-digit inflation, crippling mortgage rates, and an unemployment rate of 8 percent. Overseas, 53 American hostages still remained captive in Iran. Sensing victory, the Republicans nominated Ronald Reagan as their party's presidential nominee. Supported by the resurgent conservative movement, Reagan won a convincing victory over Jimmy Carter.

REAGANOMICS

1. President Reagan inherited a struggling economy. Unlike New Deal and Great Society reformers, Reagan did not propose a package of expensive government programs. Instead, he reversed generations of liberal economic practices by declaring, "Government is not the solution to our problems. Government is the problem."

2. Reagan proposed a Program for Economic Recovery that reporters promptly labelled "REAGANOMICS." The president's economic plan included three fundamental goals. First and foremost, it called for a significant reduction in personal and corporate tax rates. Second, Reagan pledged to eliminate unnecessary and inefficient federal regulations. And finally, the president's plan asked Congress to cut $41 billion from 83 federal programs.

3. Reagan's proposal included two key exceptions. Yielding to strong public support, he promised to make no cuts in Social Security, Medicare, or veteran's pensions. In addition, Reagan called for a massive program of military spending to deter Soviet aggression.

4. Reagan's program of cutting taxes and deregulating many industries helped restore economic prosperity. However, his massive defense budgets led to dramatic increases in the national debt.

THE END OF THE COLD WAR

1. America's relationship with the Soviet Union dominated Reagan's foreign policy. In a speech given on March 8, 1983, Reagan charged the Soviet Union with being "the focus of evil in the modern world." Reagan's "Evil Empire" speech inspired dissidents behind the Iron Curtain.

2. President Reagan did more than give speeches lambasting the Soviet Union. He also launched a massive military buildup by increasing annual defense budgets from $144 billion to $295 billion.

3. America's growing military strength alarmed Soviet leaders. They recognized that their faltering economy could not match America's scientific and technological advantages.

4. Reagan's confrontational approach to the Soviet Union began to change when Mikhail Gorbachev assumed power in 1985. The new Soviet leader initiated an ambitious program of reforms aimed at opening the Soviet system and restructuring its economy.

5. Although Reagan and Gorbachev remained ideological adversaries, they nonetheless agreed to a series of arms control agreements. As tensions between the two superpowers eased, Gorbachev began to relax the Soviet Union's grip on Eastern Europe.

6. President George H.W. Bush proved to be a skillful and patient diplomat. His administration witnessed the fall of the Berlin Wall (1989) and the collapse of the Soviet Union (1991). President Bush hailed these historic events as the beginning of a "new world order."

A CHANGING ECONOMY

1. The Berlin Wall fell on November 9, 1989. The momentous event received worldwide attention from newspaper headlines, television reports, and radio broadcasts. However, no one could use Google to search for information, like a Facebook picture of the jubilant crowds in Berlin, or use an iPhone to send a text message to a friend. Yet, in just twenty years, all of these activities became indispensable parts of a historic digital revolution.

2. The age of personal computers began in June 1977 when the newly formed Apple Company first marketed its Apple II computer. Four years later, IBM launched its first PC, or personal computer. Led by Apple and IBM, the new generation of computers used microprocessors to drastically reduce computer size while enabling users to read, write, and calculate at unprecedented speeds.

3. Prior to the early 1990s, individual computer operators could not make electronic connections with other users. Introduced during the mid-1990s, the Internet created a system of interconnected computers, allowing individuals to share, seek, and compile information.

4. The smartphone revolution began on January 9, 2007, when Steve Jobs boldly proclaimed, "Today, Apple is going to reinvent the phone." Jobs wasn't exaggerating; Apple's new iPhone began a revolution in mobile technology that is still transforming daily life throughout the world.

5. The digital revolution dramatically accelerated the global movement of goods, workers, and capital. The process by which the world's economies are becoming more integrated and interdependent is known as GLOBALIZATION.

6. Manufacturing jobs constituted the core of America's industrial economy from the 1950s to the 1980s. However, employment in manufacturing peaked in 1979. During the next four decades America lost over 7 million manufacturing jobs.

7. Many economists pointed to automation as a major reason why America lost so many manufacturing jobs. They noted that during the 1980s automobile companies began using robots to automate their assembly lines. Other manufacturers soon found that robots were effective, cost-efficient, and safe.

8. While they did not dispute the importance of automation, a growing number of economists pointed to globalization as an additional reason for the loss of American manufacturing jobs. As worldwide competition for low-cost labor intensified, a number of American companies relocated their production facilities to China and Mexico. For example, Apple engineers designed the iPhone at the company's headquarters in Cupertino, California. However, the device is assembled by hundreds of thousands of poorly paid workers in massive factories in China.

9. The digital revolution and globalization are transforming the American economy. As the manufacturing sector has declined, membership in unions has steadily fallen. At the same time, competition with global workers has produced relentless downward pressure on the real wages earned by many working- and middle-class Americans.

10. Government statistics document a widening income inequality. Between 1980 and 2012, the share of aggregate income earned by the top 1 percent rose from 8.2 percent to 19.3 percent. During this same time, middle-class incomes stagnated, while the shares of aggregate income earned by the lowest fifth fell from 4.2 percent to 3.2 percent.

MIGRATION AND IMMIGRATION IN THE 1990S AND 2000S

1. The Baby Boom generation includes 76 million people born between 1946 and 1964. As the Baby Boomers began to retire, they put increasing financial pressure on the Social Security System.

2. By 2000, a majority of Americans lived in the Sunbelt states. California, Texas, and Florida now rank as America's three most populous states. The region's surging population growth has given Sunbelt states a greater voice in presidential elections and national political issues.

3. The Immigration Act of 1965 triggered a major new wave of immigration to America. Between 1990 and 2000, over 10 million immigrants entered the United States. The largest number came from Latin America and Asia.

CHALLENGES OF THE 21ST CENTURY

1. On the morning of September 11, 2001, nineteen Islamic terrorists hijacked four U.S airliners. The terrorists slammed two planes into the twin towers of the World Trade Center in New York City and a third into the Pentagon. The fourth plane crashed on a field in southern Pennsylvania after heroic passengers attacked the hijackers. The attacks claimed the lives of over 3,000 innocent victims and first responders.

2. President George W. Bush vowed the United States would "hunt down and punish" those responsible for the 9/11 attacks. The war on terrorism led to lengthy, controversial conflicts in Afghanistan and Iraq.

3. The war on terrorism also led to new security measures in the United States. President George W. Bush signed the USA Patriot Act into law on October 26, 2001. The act gave the federal government broad powers to combat terrorism by making it easier for law enforcement agencies to search the medical, telephone, and financial records of suspected terrorists. Critics argued that the law's new security measures often conflicted with America's traditional respect for civil liberties.

4. Full-body scans at airports and security threats posed by sleeper cells and lone-wolf attackers have all become part of the post-9/11 American psyche. Long accustomed to living in a secure homeland, Americans now knew that despite their general happiness, the United States is no longer completely safe.

5. Although the United States faced continuing economic and political challenges, America continued as the world's leading superpower.

CHAPTER 10
MAKING COMPARISONS

PERIOD 1: 1491 – 1607

1. Along the Pacific coast, the hunting-gathering-fishing complex was so productive that native peoples did not feel the pressures to practice horticulture that existed among early peoples in the Desert Southwest.

2. No Native Americans possessed an ideology that impelled them far beyond their known world in search of new lands and people to conquer and exploit. In contrast, imperial rivalries, religious ideologies, and the economic pressures of mercantile capitalism drove European nations to search for new trade routes to Asia.

3. Compared with Europeans, Native Americans carried a more limited and less deadly array of pathogenic microbes.

PERIOD 2: 1607 – 1754

1. The Spanish more actively sought to convert indigenous peoples to Christianity than did the English.

2. The population in colonial New England was larger and more gender-balanced than the population in New France.

3. English settlements in Virginia and Maryland had a lower life expectancy, larger population of indentured servants, and a greater gender imbalance than the English settlements in New England.

4. The relationship between Native Americans and the French was most similar to the relationship between Native Americans and the Dutch.

5. Spain exercised greater royal control over its New World colonies than the control exercised by English royal authorities over their North American colonies.

6. English colonists were typically Protestants while Spanish colonists were overwhelmingly Catholics.

7. New England colonies relied upon a mixed economy based upon fishing, lumber, and small farming, while the Chesapeake colonies relied upon cash crops and slave labor.

8. Virginia was founded by a joint-stock company hoping to make a profit, while the New England colonies were founded by religious dissidents seeking greater freedom of religion.

9. The Middle Colonies were more urban and had more port cities than the more rural Chesapeake colonies.

10.　Plantations devoted to producing cash crops dominated the economies of both the British West Indies and the Chesapeake colonies. Planters in the British West Indies produced sugar, while those in the Chesapeake produced tobacco. Planters in both regions relied upon the labor of enslaved Africans.

PERIOD 3: 1754 – 1800

1. The ideas about government expressed in Paine's "Common Sense" and Jefferson's Declaration of Independence are most consistent with ideas about the rights of individuals and republican self-government expressed by John Locke and other Enlightenment writers.

2. Washington's Farewell Address recommendation that the United States should avoid entangling foreign alliances strongly influenced senators who opposed joining the League of Nations.

PERIOD 4: 1800 – 1848

1. Both the Erie Canal and the first transcontinental railroad reduced shipping times and opened access to more interconnected markets.

2. The South relied much less on wage labor than the Northeast.

3. The North was more integrated with the rest of the nation than the South due to internal improvements such as canals, roads, and railroad.

4. Both the Northwest Ordinance of 1787 and the Missouri Compromise of 1820 asserted the right of the federal government to restrict the territorial expansion of slavery.

5. Northern reformers initiated anti-slavery movements in both 1780 – 1810 and in 1830 – 1859. In both time periods, Northern reformers viewed slavery as a moral sin that tarnished America's new democratic republic.

6. The arguments expressed in the South Carolina Ordinance of Nullification were similar to arguments expressed by Southern states as they seceded from the Union.

7. The wave of Irish immigrants in the 1840s and the wave of New Immigrants in the 1890s both sparked an upsurge of nativist sentiment.

8. The language and themes in the Declaration of Independence inspired the ideas and goals expressed in the Seneca Falls Declaration of Sentiments and Resolutions.

9. Under republican motherhood, women were indirectly involved in politics through their roles as mothers and educators. In contrast, women at the Seneca Falls Convention demanded a direct civic voice through voting.

10. Both the ideas of republican motherhood and the ideas of the Seneca Falls convention appealed to middle-class White women.

PERIOD 5: 1844 – 1876

1. Settlement patterns in colonial America and in the western territories triggered conflict between White settlers and Native Americans over landownership.

2. Both Populists and Progressives favored a stronger federal role in the U.S. economic system.

3. Women participated in the temperance movement and other reform efforts during both the Second Great Awakening and the Progressive Era.

4. The Gospel of Wealth asserted that the wealthy have a moral responsibility to help the less fortunate and improve society. In contrast, advocates of the Social Gospel believed Christians have a moral responsibility to actively confront poverty and other social problems.

5. Wood served as the primary energy source during the Market Revolution. In contrast, coal served as the primary energy source during the Second Industrial Revolution. Coal powered trains and fueled the mass production of steel.

PERIOD 7: 1890 – 1945

1. The federal government used its legal authority to address threats considered a clear and present danger during the Red Scare after World War I and after the 9/11 terrorist attacks.

2. Booker T. Washington urged African Americans to follow a policy of accommodation by accepting segregation, avoiding political agitation, and concentrating on economic advancement. In contrast, W.E.B. Du Bois urged African Americans to follow a policy of "ceaseless agitation" to

challenge Jim Crow segregation and demand full economic, social, and political equality.

3. Both Marcus Garvey and Malcolm X emphasized racial pride and economic self-sufficiency.

4. The passage of the Nineteenth Amendment eliminated sex discrimination in voting. This enabled women of the 1920s to take more active roles in the political life of their communities and states.

PERIOD 8: 1945 - 1980

1. Fear and anxiety caused by the spread of international communism sparked Red Scares following both World War I and World War II.

2. The United States became involved in both the Korean War and the Vietnam War to fulfill its policy of containment.

3. Public opposition was more significant for the Vietnam War than for the Korean War. The Vietnam War sparked a massive anti-war movement that led to an increasingly polarized society in which "doves" opposed the Vietnam War and "hawks" supported it.

4. Both the 1920s and the 1950s witnessed the growth of robust consumer cultures supported by mass advertising and booming economies.

5. A Great Migration of African Americans from the rural South to cities in the North, Midwest, and West took place in the period from 1910 to 1930 and the period from 1941 to 1980. African Americans in both periods moved to escape discrimination and pursue economic opportunity.

6. The New Deal sought to stabilize capitalism and stave off the return of the Great Depression. In contrast, the Great Society sought to extend the benefits of affluence to all Americans and to eradicate poverty.

7. The New Deal did not address institutional discrimination against African Americans. In contrast, the Great Society included landmark legislation that banned segregation in public facilities and outlawed practices used to block black people from voting.

8. Following the Seneca Falls Convention, the first wave of feminist activism focused on winning the right to vote. During the 1960s and 1970s, a second wave of feminist activism focused on achieving equal opportunities in education and employment, accessible and affordable childcare, and the right to safe and legal abortions.

PERIOD 9: 1980 – 2010

1. President Reagan's supply-side economic policies were similar to the laissez-faire economic policies followed by President Coolidge during the 1920s.

2. Both President Kennedy and President Reagan used forceful speeches at the Berlin Wall to condemn the Soviet Union. Standing on a platform near the Berlin Wall, President Kennedy declared, "All free men, wherever they may live, are citizens of Berlin, and therefore, as a free man, I take pride in the words, Ich bin ein Berliner!" Almost 24 years later, President Reagan stood near the Berlin Wall and boldly declared, "Mr. Gorbachev, tear down this wall."

3. The process of globalization began when Columbus's small fleet of three ships began exploring the Caribbean islands and set in motion a complex movement of people, foods, animals, and germs known as the Columbian Exchange. Today, the ongoing digital revolution is dramatically accelerating the global movement of people, products, and ideas.

GLOSSARY
KEY TERMS AND HISTORIC GENERALIZATIONS
YOU ABSOLUTELY, POSITIVELY HAVE
TO KNOW

The glossaries in APUSH textbooks and prep books contain hundreds of vocabulary terms. If all of these words had an equal chance of appearing on your APUSH exam, studying would be very time-consuming and tedious.

Fortunately, the College Board provides APUSH students and teachers with a definitive course Framework. You can find this document at the AP Central website. The Framework provides a definitive presentation of the key terms and historic generalizations that form the backbone of the APUSH course. All of the questions on your APUSH exam are anchored in the course Framework.

The terms and generalizations featured in this Glossary are all derived from the APUSH Framework and are covered in Chapters 1–10. That is why you absolutely, positively have to know this essential content. It will make a significant contribution to your APUSH score!

1. BABY BOOM – The postwar marriage boom triggered a tidal wave of 76 million births from 1946 to 1964. The size of the baby boom cohort contributed to the economic boom of the 1950s and the rise of a youth culture during the 1960s.

2. BEATS – A small but influential group of literary figures based in New York City and San Francisco in the 1950s. Beat writers felt alienated from America's excessive materialism and constant pressure to get along.

3. BLACK POWER – Led by Malcolm X and Stokely Carmichael, Black Power advocates urged African Americans to build economic and political power by forming black-owned businesses and voting for black candidates for political offices.

4. COLD WAR – The prolonged period of economic and political rivalry between the United States and the Soviet Union.

5. COLLECTIVE SECURITY – A principle of mutual support in which all nations in an alliance pledge to consider an attack on one as an attack on all.

6. COLUMBIAN EXCHANGE – The exchange of plants, animals, microbes, and peoples between the New World, Europe, and Africa in the 150 years following the discovery of America in 1492.

7. CONSERVATIONISTS – Believed government policies should promote the management of natural resources in a responsible and sustained manner.

8. CONTAINMENT – America's Cold War strategy of blocking the expansion of Soviet influence.

9. COUNTERCULTURE – A cultural movement during the late 1960s associated with an alternative lifestyle based upon peace, love, and "doing your own thing."

10. CULT OF DOMESTICITY – The idealization of women in their roles as wives and mothers. As a nurturing mother and faithful spouse, the wife had a special responsibility to create a home that was a "haven in a heartless world."

11. DÉTENTE – A policy advocated by President Nixon to relax tensions between the United States and the Soviet Union. Examples of détente include Nixon's trip to Moscow, the signing of a Strategic Arms Limitation Treaty, expanded trade with Russia, and joint U.S. and Soviet space missions.

12. DOMINO THEORY – Geopolitical belief that the fall of South Vietnam to communism would inevitably lead to Communist expansion throughout the rest of Southeast Asia.

13. ENCOMIENDA – A license granted by the Spanish to royal officials to extract labor and tribute from native peoples in specific areas.

14. ENLIGHTENMENT – An eighteenth-century philosophical movement that emphasized the use of reason to question previously accepted doctrines and traditions. Leading Enlightenment thinkers stressed that all people have natural rights to life, liberty, and property.

15. FIRST GREAT AWAKENING – A period of intense religious revival that began in New England in the mid-1730s and then spread across all the colonies by the 1740s. The First Great Awakening stressed emotion as a way to achieve personal salvation.

16. FLAPPERS – Young women in the 1920s who defied conventional standards of conduct by wearing short skirts and makeup, dancing to jazz, and flaunting a liberated lifestyle.

17. FORCED ASSIMILATION – Policy pursued by the Bureau of Indian Affairs to "Americanize" Native American children.

18.   GLOBALIZATION – The process by which technological, economic, political, and cultural exchanges are making the world more interconnected and interdependent. As a result, the United States is now part of an integrated global economy.

19.   GREAT MIGRATION – The mass movement of African Americans from the rural South to cities in the North, Midwest, and West Coast. The Great Migration began slowly in 1910 and accelerated between the First World War and the Great Crash. A second wave occurred in the two decades following the Second World War.

20.   HARLEM RENAISSANCE – An outpouring of literature and art by African American writers and artists during the 1920s. Harlem Renaissance writers used the term "New Negro" as a proud assertion of their African American heritage and culture.

21.   IMPERIALISM – The policy of extending a nation's power through military conquest, economic domination, and/or territorial annexation.

22.   ISOLATIONISM – A U.S. foreign policy calling for America to avoid entangling alliances following the First World War. During the 1930s, isolationists drew support from ideas expressed in Washington's Farewell Address. The Neutrality Acts of the 1930s were expressions of a commitment to isolationism.

23.   JUDICIAL REVIEW – The power of the Supreme Court to strike down an act of Congress as unconstitutional. Established by the Marshall Court in *Marbury v. Madison*.

24.   MANIFEST DESTINY – Nineteenth-century belief that the United States was destined to spread democratic institutions and the blessings of liberty across the North American continent.

25.   McCARTHYISM – Term associated with Senator Joseph McCarthy's anticommunist crusade during the early 1950s. McCarthy's campaign of innuendo and half-truths made him one of the most feared and powerful politicians in America. The political climate of the McCarthy years resembled the attacks on radicals and immigrants following the First World War.

26.   MERCANTILISM – A British economic policy designed to achieve a favorable balance of trade by exporting more goods than it imported. In order to achieve this goal, Great Britain purchased raw materials from its American colonies and then sold them more expensive manufactured goods.

27.   MUCKRAKERS – Progressive Era journalists who exposed illegal business practices, social injustices, and corrupt urban political bosses.

28.   NATIVIST – Anti-foreign sentiment favoring the interests of native-born people over the interests of immigrants. Nativism directed against Irish and German immigrants in the 1840s and 1850s fueled the rise of the Know-Nothing Party. Nativism reappeared as a reaction to the mass immigration from Eastern and Southern Europe between 1890 and 1920.

29.   NEW IMMIGRANTS – The massive wave of immigrants from Southern and Eastern Europe who came to America between 1890 and 1924. Booming industrial growth offered the immigrants plentiful jobs, while America's constitutional freedoms offered them hope for new lives.

30.   PERFECTIONISM – Belief that people can achieve a moral perfection in their earthly lives. Perfectionism led to an optimistic faith in the human ability to build a just society.

31.   PRESERVATIONISTS – Believed government policies should preserve wilderness areas in their natural state.

32.   PROGRESSIVES – Predominantly well-educated, middle-class reformers who lived in urban areas. Middle-class women played a leading role in the Progressive movement. Progressives wanted the government to play an active role in eliminating industrial abuses, expanding democratic practices, and supporting moral reform. However, Progressives devoted little attention to the plight of African Americans.

33.   POPULAR SOVEREIGNTY – Belief that the settlers in a given territory have the right to decide whether or not to accept slavery.

34.   REAGONOMICS - Term used by the press to describe President Reagan's economic policies. Reagan's program attempted to promote growth and investment by deregulating business, reducing corporate tax rates, and lowering federal taxes for upper-income and middle-income Americans.

35.   RED SCARE –Wave of anticommunist hysteria that swept across the United States after World War I.

36.   REPUBLICANISM – The belief that government should be based on the consent of the governed. Republicanism was a key part of the revolutionary spirit that motivated colonial resistance to Britain's arbitrary taxation.

37.   REPUBLICAN MOTHERHOOD – The idea that American mothers have the important responsibility of becoming exemplary parents who would raise their children to become virtuous citizens. Women would thus play a vital role in shaping America's moral character.

38.   SECOND GREAT AWAKENING – A wave of religious fervor that swept across America between 1800 and 1830. Leading Second Great Awakening ministers such as Charles Grandison Finney delivered inspiring sermons

stressing that Christians are "moral free agents" who could achieve personal salvation and thus spiritual rebirth.

39.   SHARECROPPING – Labor system in which newly freed slaves exchanged their labor for the use of the planter's land, tools, and seed. The sharecropper typically gave the landowner half of the crops as payment for the use of his property. The system trapped African Americans in a seemingly endless cycle of poverty and debt.

40.   SOCIAL DARWINISM – The belief that there is a natural evolutionary process by which the fittest will survive and prosper. During the Gilded Age, wealthy business and industrial leaders used Social Darwinism to explain and justify their great wealth.

41.   SOCIAL GOSPEL – Late nineteenth-century reform movement based on the belief that Christians have a moral responsibility to actively confront poverty and other social problems.

42.   STAGFLATION – The simultaneous occurrence of rising unemployment and double-digit inflation that plagued the U.S. economy during the late 1970s.

43.   SUNBELT – A booming region of 14 states stretching from North Carolina through Florida and Texas to Arizona and California. Sunbelt conservatives formed an important part of the coalition that helped elect Ronald Reagan president in 1980.

44.   TRANSCENDENTALISM – A philosophical and literary movement that stressed the importance of intuition, nonconformity, and the belief that truth could be found in nature. Ralph Waldo Emerson, Henry David Thoreau, and Margaret Fuller were the leading transcendentalists.

45.   VIETNAMIZATION – Nixon's policy of training South Vietnamese soldiers to take the place of withdrawing American forces.

Made in the USA
Columbia, SC
23 March 2021

34928435R00083